혼공

중학 영문법 마스터

Level

1

혼공북스

이 책의 구성과 특징

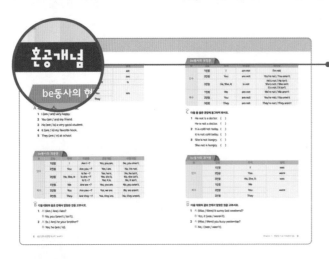

1 문법 개념 확인

문법 설명에서 꼭 배워야 할 핵심 내용을 도표로 정리했습니다. 각 개념을 배운 후에는 연계 문제를 통해 복습할 수 있습니다.

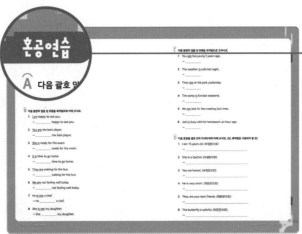

2 학습한 문법 내용 적용

'혼공개념'에서 학습한 문법에 대한 이해도를 점검할 수 있는 문제로 구성했습니다. 가장 기초적인 연습 문제를 통해 학습한 개념을 바로 확인해 볼 수 있습니다.

3 대표 기출 유형 연습

'혼공연습'에서 한 걸음 나아간 문제로 구성했습니다. 학습한 문법 개념들을 본격적으로 적용해 볼 수 있는 단계별 문제를 통해, 개념을 정확하게 이해할 수 있도록 구성했습니다.

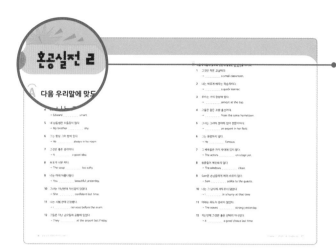

4 서술형 평가 완성

서술형 평가에 대비할 수 있도록 빈칸에 알맞은 단어를 채우고, 문장을 영작할 수 있는 문제로 구성했습니다. 문법 개념을 이해하는 것뿐 아니라 쓰기에서도 활용하며 확실히 습득할 수 있습니다.

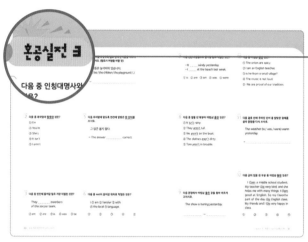

5 학교 시험 완벽 대비

각 챕터에서 배운 내용을 바탕으로 객관식, 주관식, 서술형, 독해 문제를 구성했습니다. 문제를 풀며 자신의 강점과 약점을 스스로 평가하고 학교 시험 실전 감각을 키울 수 있습니다.

무료 동영상 강의 제공

400만 명의 수강생이 선택한 EBS 인기 강사 혼공쌤의 강의 32강을 무료로 수강할 수 있습니다.

유쾌한 혼공쌤의 강의를 통해 진정한 **중학 영문법 마스터**가 되어 보세요!

차례

CHAPTER

1

문장의 기초 1
(be동사 편)

- be동사의 현재형
- be동사의 의문문
- be동사의 부정문
- be동사의 과거형

be동사의 현재형

수	인칭	주어	형태
단수	1인칭	I	am
	2인칭	You	are
	3인칭	He, She, It	is
복수	1인칭	We	
	2인칭	You	are
	3인칭	They	

A 다음 괄호 안에서 알맞은 것을 고르시오.

1 I (am / are) very happy.

2 You (am / are) my friend.

3 He (are / is) a very good student.

4 It (are / is) my favorite book.

5 They (are / is) at school.

be동사의 의문문

수	인칭	주어	의문문	긍정 대답	부정 대답
단수	1인칭	I	Am I ~?	Yes, you are.	No, you aren't.
	2인칭	You	Are you ~?	Yes, I am.	No, I'm not.
	3인칭	He, She, It	Is he ~? Is she ~? Is it ~?	Yes, he is. Yes, she is. Yes, it is.	No, he isn't. No, she isn't. No, it isn't.
복수	1인칭	We	Are we ~?	Yes, you are.	No, you aren't.
	2인칭	You	Are you ~?	Yes, we are.	No, we aren't.
	3인칭	They	Are they ~?	Yes, they are.	No, they aren't.

B 다음 대화의 괄호 안에서 알맞은 것을 고르시오.

1 A: (Am / Are) I late?

   B: No, you (aren't / isn't).

2 A: (Is / Are) he your brother?

   B: Yes, he (are / is).

be동사의 부정문

수	인칭	주어	부정문	축약형
단수	1인칭	I	am not	I'm not
	2인칭	You	are not	You're not / You aren't
	3인칭	He, She, It	is not	He's not / He isn't She's not / She isn't It's not / It isn't
복수	1인칭	We	are not	We're not / We aren't
	2인칭	You	are not	You're not / You aren't
	3인칭	They	are not	They're not / They aren't

C 다음 중 옳은 문장에 동그라미 하시오.

1 He not is a doctor. (   )

   He is not a doctor. (   )

2 It is cold not today. (   )

   It is not cold today. (   )

3 She is not hungry. (   )

   She not is hungry. (   )

be동사의 과거형

수	인칭	주어	형태
단수	1인칭	I	was
	2인칭	You	were
	3인칭	He, She, It	was
복수	1인칭	We	were
	2인칭	You	
	3인칭	They	

D 다음 대화의 괄호 안에서 알맞은 것을 고르시오.

1 A: (Was / Were) it sunny last weekend?

   B: Yes, it (was / weren't).

2 A: (Was / Were) you busy yesterday?

   B: No, I (was / wasn't).

A 다음 괄호 안에서 알맞은 것을 고르시오.

1 I (am / are) at home.

2 We (is / are) friends.

3 You (is / are) a good singer.

4 It (am / is) funny.

5 The room (is / are) clean.

6 The cups (am / are) on the table.

7 My sister (is / are) tall.

8 They (is / are) in the garden.

B 다음 문장의 밑줄 친 부분을 축약형으로 바꿔 쓰시오.

1 <u>I am</u> happy to see you.

→ _____ happy to see you.

2 <u>You are</u> the best player.

→ _____ the best player.

3 <u>She is</u> ready for the exam.

→ _____ ready for the exam.

4 <u>It is</u> time to go home.

→ _____ time to go home.

5 <u>They are</u> waiting for the bus.

→ _____ waiting for the bus.

6 <u>We are</u> not feeling well today.

→ _____ not feeling well today.

7 He <u>is not</u> a chef.

→ He _____ a chef.

8 She <u>is not</u> my daughter.

→ She _____ my daughter.

C 다음 문장의 밑줄 친 부분을 과거형으로 고치시오.

1 You <u>are</u> too young 5 years ago.

→ _____

2 The weather <u>is</u> cold last night.

→ _____

3 They <u>are</u> at the park yesterday.

→ _____

4 The party <u>is</u> fun last weekend.

→ _____

5 We <u>are</u> late for the meeting last time.

→ _____

6 Joel <u>is</u> busy with his homework an hour ago.

→ _____

D 다음 문장을 괄호 안의 지시에 따라 바꿔 쓰시오. (단, 축약형은 사용하지 말 것)

1 I am 15 years old. (부정문으로)

→ _____

2 She is a teacher. (부정문으로)

→ _____

3 You are honest. (부정문으로)

→ _____

4 He is very smart. (의문문으로)

→ _____

5 They are your best friends. (의문문으로)

→ _____

6 The butterfly is colorful. (의문문으로)

→ _____

A 다음 괄호 안에서 알맞은 것을 고르시오.

1   I (am / are) okay.

2   You (is / are) a scientist.

3   It (is / are) a surprise party.

4   Tom (is / are) busy today.

5   She (is / are) scared.

6   He (is / are) calm.

7   You (is / are) important to me.

8   The test (is / are) easy.

9   She (is / are) in the living room.

10   Suji and John (is / are) friends.

11   He (is / are) in art class.

12   They (is / are) in the library.

13   Students (is / are) in the classroom.

14   You (is / are) so kind.

15   They (is / are) helpful.

16   The musicians (is / are) popular.

17   He (is / are) a lawyer.

18   It (is / are) interesting.

19   People (is / are) all different.

20   My mom and I (am / are) in the kitchen.

B 다음 괄호 안에서 알맞은 것을 고르시오.

1   He (is / was) here yesterday.

2   She (is / was) tired last night.

3   You (are / were) ready now.

4   He (is / was) angry last time.

5   She (is / was) sad yesterday.

6   They (aren't / weren't) outside last Saturday.

7   She (is / was) in France last summer.

8   I (am / was) busy last weekend.

9   It (is / was) quiet now.

10 She (is / was) on the team last season.

11 It (is / was) snowy last Friday.

12 It (is / was) cold outside now.

13 She (was / were) absent yesterday.

14 I (am / was) a new student last year.

15 The weather (is / was) very hot last summer.

16 It (is / was) a holiday the day before yesterday.

17 We (was / were) classmates 2 years ago.

18 We (are / were) on vacation last winter.

19 He (was / were) an actor in the 1990s.

20 She (wasn't / weren't) at the mall an hour ago.

C 다음 괄호 안에서 알맞은 것을 고르시오.

1 I (amn't / am not) a swimmer.

2 You (aren't / isn't) a member of the team.

3 He (aren't / isn't) a nurse at the hospital.

4 The seats (aren't / isn't) clean.

5 The driver (aren't / isn't) friendly.

6 The store (isn't / aren't) open yet.

7 These shoes (isn't / aren't) on sale.

8 The food court (isn't / aren't) crowded today.

9 Mike (isn't / aren't) the owner of the car.

10 (I'm not / I amn't) interested in this.

11 The tickets (isn't / aren't) cheap here.

12 The food (aren't / isn't) very hot.

13 The waiter in the restaurant (isn't / aren't) kind.

14 She (aren't / isn't) proud of the team.

15 We (aren't / isn't) in the waiting room.

16 I (wasn't / weren't) at home yesterday.

17 The ambulance (wasn't / weren't) here quickly.

18 They (wasn't / weren't) the champions last year.

19 You (aren't / weren't) at the swimming pool yesterday.

20 They (aren't / weren't) on the soccer field last night.

D 다음 대화의 괄호 안에서 알맞은 것을 고르시오.

1 A: (Am / Are) you a basketball player?

B: No, I (am / am not).

2 A: (Is / Are) he your brother?

B: Yes, he (are / is).

3 A: (Is / Are) you on the subway?

B: Yes, I (am / is).

4 A: (Is / Are) this your book?

B: No, it (is / isn't).

5 A: (Are / Is) we in the right classroom?

B: Yes, we (are / aren't).

6 A: (Is / Are) the library open now?

B: Yes, it (is / are).

7 A: (Is / Are) the water warm?

B: No, it (is / isn't).

8 A: (Is / Are) the shoes dirty?

B: No, they (are / aren't).

9 A: (Is / Are) the lake in the park deep?

B: Yes, it (is / are).

혼공실전 2

A 다음 우리말에 맞도록 빈칸에 알맞은 단어를 쓰시오.

1 나는 작가이다.

→ I _____ a writer.

2 우리는 예술가이다.

→ We _____ artists.

3 당신은 용감하다.

→ You _____ brave.

4 Edward는 똑똑하다.

→ Edward _____ smart.

5 내 남동생은 수줍음이 많다.

→ My brother _____ shy.

6 그는 항상 그의 방에 있다.

→ He _____ always in his room.

7 그것은 좋은 생각이다.

→ It _____ a good idea.

8 수프가 너무 짜다.

→ The soup _____ too salty.

9 너는 어제 아름다웠다.

→ You _____ beautiful yesterday.

10 그녀는 지난번에 자신감이 있었다.

→ She _____ confident last time.

11 나는 시험 전에 긴장했다.

→ I _____ nervous before the exam.

12 그들은 지난 금요일에 공항에 있었다.

→ They _____ at the airport last Friday.

B 다음 우리말에 맞도록 빈칸에 알맞은 <u>한 단어</u>를 쓰시오.

1   그것은 작은 교실이다.

→ _____ a small classroom.

2   너는 빠르게 배우는 학습자이다.

→ _____ a quick learner.

3   우리는 거의 정상에 있다.

→ _____ almost at the top.

4   그들은 같은 고향 출신이다.

→ _____ from the same hometown.

5   그녀는 그녀의 분야에 있어 전문가이다.

→ _____ an expert in her field.

6   그는 유명하지 않다.

→ He _____ famous.

7   그 배우들은 아직 무대에 있지 않다.

→ The actors _____ on stage yet.

8   창문들이 깨끗하지 않다.

→ The windows _____ clean.

9   Sam은 손님들에게 예의 바르지 않다.

→ Sam _____ polite to the guests.

10   나는 그 당시에 서두르지 않았다.

→ I _____ in a hurry at that time.

11   어제는 파도가 강하지 않았다.

→ The waves _____ strong yesterday.

12   지난번에 그것은 좋은 선택이 아니었다.

→ It _____ a good choice last time.

C 다음 문장을 부정문으로 바꿔 쓰시오.

1 You are healthy.

→ _____

2 I am angry today.

→ _____

3 She is a math teacher.

→ _____

4 We are students.

→ _____

5 The sky is blue.

→ _____

6 They are neighbors.

→ _____

7 The book is interesting.

→ _____

8 The workers are in a new house.

→ _____

9 They are members of the science club.

→ _____

10 The food was good.

→ _____

11 The lights were out.

→ _____

12 The truck was in the parking lot.

→ _____

13 I was curious about the new project.

→ _____

14 He was with his friends at the mall.

→ _____

15 She was excited about her new job.

→ _____

D 다음 문장을 의문문으로 바꿔 쓰시오.

1   The room is too small.

    → _____

2   The carts are full.

    → _____

3   The line is long.

    → _____

4   The books are on the shelf.

    → _____

5   She was not at school yesterday.

    → _____

6   She is always helpful to everyone.

    → _____

7   The students were ready for the trip.

    → _____

8   You are important to your family.

    → _____

9   She is very happy with her job.

    → _____

10 The teacher was very friendly.

    → _____

11 The bugs were active after rain.

    → _____

12 It was a beautiful day for a picnic.

    → _____

13 I was in the bookstore for hours.

    → _____

14 The chairs were comfortable.

    → _____

15 She was thirsty from walking under the hot sun.

    → _____

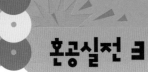

혼공실전 ㅋ

1 다음 중 인칭대명사와 be동사가 잘못 짝지어진 것은?

① I - am

② You - are

③ He - is

④ She - is

⑤ We - is

2 다음 중 축약형이 잘못된 것은?

① I'm

② You're

③ She's

④ It isn't

⑤ I amn't

3 다음 중 빈칸에 들어갈 말로 가장 적절한 것은?

> They _____ members
> of the soccer team.

① am ② are ③ is ④ was ⑤ be

4 다음 우리말에 맞도록 괄호 안의 단어들을 바르게 배열하시오. (필요시 어형을 바꿀 것)

> 아이들은 놀이터에 있습니다.
> (in / be / the children / the playground / .)

→ _____

5 다음 우리말에 맞도록 빈칸에 알맞은 한 단어를 쓰시오.

> 그 답은 옳지 않다.

→ The answer _____ correct.

6 다음 중 not이 들어갈 위치로 적절한 것은?

> I ① am ② familiar ③ with
> ④ the local ⑤ language.

①   ②   ③   ④   ⑤

7 다음 빈칸에 공통으로 들어갈 말로 적절한 것은?

- It _____ windy yesterday.
- I _____ at the beach last week.

① is ② are ③ am ④ was ⑤ were

8 다음 중 밑줄 친 부분이 어법상 틀린 것은?

① It <u>isn't</u> rainy.
② They <u>aren't</u> tall.
③ We <u>aren't</u> on the boat.
④ The clothes <u>aren't</u> dirty.
⑤ Tom <u>aren't</u> in trouble.

9 다음 문장에서 어법상 틀린 곳을 찾아 바르게 고치시오.

The show is boring yesterday.

_____ → _____

10 다음 중 어법상 틀린 것은?

① The onion are spicy.
② I am an English teacher.
③ Is he from a small village?
④ The music is not loud.
⑤ We are proud of our tradition.

11 다음 괄호 안에 주어진 단어 중 알맞은 형태를 골라 문장을 다시 쓰시오.

The weather (is / was / were) warm yesterday.

→ _____

12 다음 글의 밑줄 친 부분 중 어법상 틀린 것은?

I ①<u>am</u> a middle school student. My teacher ②<u>is</u> very kind, and she helps me with many things. I ③<u>am</u> good at English. So my favorite part of the day ④<u>is</u> English class. My friends and I ⑤<u>is</u> very happy in class.

①   ②   ③   ④   ⑤

[13-15] 다음 우리말에 맞도록 빈칸에 알맞은 말을 보기 에서 골라 쓰시오.

보기 am   are   is   isn't   aren't

13

나는 테니스 선수이다.

→ I _____ a tennis player.

14

그 차는 당장 이용 가능하지 않다.

→ The car _____ available right now.

15

시험 결과가 좋니?

→ _____ the test result good?

16 다음 대화의 빈칸에 들어갈 말로 적절한 것은?

A: Was your English homework difficult?
B: No, it _____.

① is
② isn't
③ was
④ wasn't
⑤ were

[17-18] 다음 대화에서 어법상 틀린 곳을 찾아 바르게 고치시오.

17

A: Are you ready to order?
B: Yes, we is.

_____ → _____

18

A: Is it so hot now?
B: Yes, it was.

_____ → _____

[19-20] 다음 문장을 의문문으로 바꿔 쓰시오.

19 He is in the office.

→ _____

20 John is interested in the game.

→ _____

21 다음 질문에 대한 대답으로 가장 적절한 것은?

> A: Was the movie good?
> B: _____

① Yes, it isn't.
② No, it wasn't.
③ Yes, they are.
④ No, they aren't.
⑤ No, it isn't.

22 다음 두 대화의 빈칸에 들어갈 말이 바르게 짝지어진 것은?

> • A: Is this computer expensive?
>   B: No, it _____.
> • A: Was your brother in his room last night?
>   B: Yes, he _____.

① is – is
② is – was
③ isn't – is
④ isn't – was
⑤ isn't – were

23 다음 글의 빈칸에 공통으로 들어갈 말로 적절한 것은?

> Once upon a time, there _____ a king. He was sad, so he tried many things. But nothing helped. One day, a kind person told him, "Happiness comes from helping others." So, the king began to help his people from his heart. He became happy. Actually, happiness _____ always in him.

① am
② are
③ is
④ was
⑤ were

2

문장의 기초 2
(일반동사 편)

· 주어의 동작이나 상태를 나타내는
  일반동사

· 일반동사의 3인칭 단수 현재형

· 일반동사의 부정문:
  주어 + do / does + not + 동사원형 ~.

· 일반동사의 의문문:
  Do / Does + 주어 + 동사원형 ~?

주어의 동작이나 상태를 나타내는 일반동사

주어		규칙
1인칭, 2인칭, 복수	I, You, We, They	동사원형
3인칭 단수	He, She, It	동사원형 + -(e)s

A 다음 문장에서 동사를 찾아 밑줄 치시오.

1 We play soccer.

2 I run every morning.

3 He reads a book.

4 She eats breakfast.

일반동사의 3인칭 단수 현재형

	규칙	예시
대부분의 동사	동사원형 + -s	work → works
-ch, -sh, -x, -s, -z, -o로 끝나는 동사	동사원형 + -es	watch → watches
동사가 자음 + -y로 끝나는 동사	y를 i로 바꾸고 + -es	study → studies
예외적인 경우	have, do	have → has do → does

B 다음 동사를 3인칭 단수 현재형으로 바꾸시오.

1 teach → _____

2 come → _____

3 try → _____

4 finish → _____

5 cry → _____

수	인칭	주어	부정형	줄임말
단수	1인칭	I	do not	I don't / You don't
	2인칭	You		
	3인칭	He, She, It	does not	He doesn't / She doesn't / It doesn't
복수	1인칭	We	do not	We don't / You don't / They don't
	2인칭	You		
	3인칭	They		

C 다음 중 옳은 문장에 동그라미 하시오.

1 I not go to school.   (   )

   I do not go to school.   (   )

2 We do like not cucumbers.   (   )

   We don't like cucumbers.   (   )

3 She doesn't like it.   (   )

   She do not like it.   (   )

수	인칭	주어	의문문	긍정 대답	부정 대답
단수	1인칭	I	Do I ~?	Yes, you do.	No, you don't.
	2인칭	You	Do you ~?	Yes, I do.	No, I don't.
	3인칭	He, She, It	Does he ~? Does she ~? Does it ~?	Yes, he does. Yes, she does. Yes, it does.	No, he doesn't. No, she doesn't. No, it doesn't.
복수	1인칭	We	Do we ~?	Yes, you do.	No, you don't.
	2인칭	You	Do you ~?	Yes, we do.	No, we don't.
	3인칭	They	Do they ~?	Yes, they do.	No, they don't.

D 다음 대화의 괄호 안에서 알맞은 것을 고르시오.

1 A: (Do / Does) you like apples?

   B: Yes, I (do / does).

2 A: (Do / Does) he go to school on foot?

   B: No, he (does / doesn't).

A 다음 괄호 안에서 알맞은 것을 고르시오.

1 She (run / runs) every morning.

2 The cats (sleep / sleeps) on the sofa.

3 She (dance / dances) at the party.

4 We (help / helps) our mom at home.

5 It (grow / grows) quickly.

6 I (paint / paints) a picture.

7 She (play / plays) the piano well.

8 It (rain / rains) a lot in the summer.

B 다음 괄호 안에서 알맞은 것을 고르시오.

1 He (go / goes) to school by bus.

2 He (do / does) his homework quickly.

3 He (studys / studies) English every day.

4 The bird (fly / flies) high in the sky.

5 She (gos / goes) to the park every morning.

6 He (trys / tries) new recipes every weekend.

7 My dad (mixs / mixes) the vegetables.

8 She (watchs / watches) TV after dinner.

C 다음 문장의 밑줄 친 부분을 축약형으로 바꿔 쓰시오.

1 I <u>do not</u> like chocolate.

→ I _____ like chocolate.

2 It <u>does not</u> have a sweet smell.

→ It _____ have a sweet smell.

3 The dog <u>does not</u> bark loudly.

→ The dog _____ bark loudly.

4 We <u>do not</u> eat lunch at 3 p.m.

→ We _____ eat lunch at 3 p.m.

5 He <u>does not</u> read a book every night.

→ He _____ read a book every night.

D 다음 문장을 괄호 안의 지시에 따라 바꿔 쓰시오.

1 He drives a blue car. (부정문으로)

→ _____

2 I sing a song at the party. (부정문으로)

→ _____

3 My dog sits on the bench. (의문문으로)

→ _____

4 She writes a letter. (의문문으로)

→ _____

5 He helps his father in the garden. (의문문으로)

→ _____

A 다음 동사의 3인칭 단수 현재형을 쓰시오.

1 play → _____

2 go → _____

3 run → _____

4 study → _____

5 watch → _____

6 fly → _____

7 read → _____

8 write → _____

9 swim → _____

10 sing → _____

11 jump → _____

12 catch → _____

13 fix → _____

14 teach → _____

15 wish → _____

16 help → _____

17 dance → _____

18 cry → _____

19 carry → _____

20 buy → _____

21 make → _____

22 eat → _____

23 laugh → _____

24 enjoy → _____

25 give → _____

26 have → _____

27 do → _____

28 say → _____

29 need → _____

30 open → _____

B 다음 괄호 안에서 알맞은 것을 고르시오.

1 We (watch / watches) TV after dinner.

2 The sun (set / sets) in the west.

3 He (fixs / fixes) his bike.

4 The bird (flyes / flies) high.

5 Her father (paint / paints) a picture.

6 My classmates (dance / dances) very well.

7 My sister and I (buy / buys) new clothes.

8 It (sound / sounds) like music.

9 A magician (shows / showes) his tricks.

10 The players (catch / catches) the ball easily.

11 He (studys / studies) hard for the test.

12 He (cook / cooks) dinner for his family.

13 I (brush / brushes) my teeth twice a day.

14 The girls (like / likes) ice cream.

15 The dog (wag / wags) its tail happily.

16 My friend (buys / buyes) a gift for me.

17 The teacher (explain / explains) the lesson clearly.

18 The rain (stops / stopps) in the afternoon.

19 You (drink / drinks) coffee every morning.

20 He and I (visit / visits) our grandparents every Sunday.

C 다음 괄호 안에서 알맞은 것을 고르시오.

1 She (don't sing / doesn't sing) beautifully.

2 We (don't run / doesn't run) every morning.

3 He (does not play / do not play) soccer.

4 The cats (don't chase / doesn't chase) the mouse.

5 My dad (don't cooks / doesn't cook) food.

6 The dog (doesn't bark / doesn't barks) at me.

7 They (do not watch / does not watch) TV every night.

8 The pigeon (doesn't fly / doesn't flies) high in the sky.

9 I (don't study / doesn't study) English every day.

10 The teacher (do not teaches / does not teach) math.

11 The brothers (don't fix / doesn't fix) their bike.

12 The boys (do not kick / does not kick) the ball hard.

13 My dad (don't drive / doesn't drive) to work.

14 The baby (don't smile / does not smile) at me.

15 He (doesn't go / doesn't goes) to the gym after work.

16 The sun (not does set / does not set) in the east.

17 She (do not writes / doesn't write) letters to her friend.

18 The clock (does not tells / does not tell) the time.

19 My mom and I (don't read / doesn't read) a book before bed.

20 He (don't love / doesn't love) playing the piano.

D 다음 대화의 괄호 안에서 알맞은 것을 고르시오.

1   A: (Are / Do) you help your friend?

    B: Yes, I (am / do).

2   A: (Does / Is) a cheetah run fast?

    B: Yes, it (is / does).

3   A: (Do / Does) he need more time?

    B: No, he (does / doesn't).

4   A: (Do / Does) the sun rise in the east?

    B: Yes, it (does / doesn't).

5   A: (Do / Does) he take a shower after jogging?

    B: Yes, he (do / does).

6   A: (Do / Does) your parents eat lunch at noon?

    B: No, they (do / don't).

7   A: (Do / Does) she know the answer to the question?

    B: No, she (don't / doesn't).

8   A: (Do / Does) your sister carry her bag to school?

    B: Yes, she (does / does not).

9   A: (Do / Does) your mom wash the dishes every night?

    B: No, she (does / doesn't).

A 다음 우리말에 맞도록 괄호 안의 단어를 이용하여 빈칸에 알맞은 말을 쓰시오. (필요시 어형을 바꿀 것)

1   나는 매일 학교에 걸어간다. (walk)

    → I _____ to school every day.

2   그들은 빨리 달린다. (run)

    → They _____ fast.

3   그녀는 학교가 끝나고 그녀의 엄마를 돕는다. (help)

    → She _____ her mom after school.

4   우리는 주말에 게임을 한다. (play)

    → We _____ games on weekends.

5   6월에는 비가 많이 내린다. (rain)

    → It _____ a lot in June.

6   Jenny는 그녀의 친구를 좋아한다. (like)

    → Jenny _____ her friend.

7   우리는 매일 수학을 공부한다. (study)

    → We _____ math every day.

8   나의 삼촌은 큰 집을 가지고 있다. (have)

    → My uncle _____ a big house.

9   그 개는 밤에 크게 짖는다. (bark)

    → The dog _____ loudly at night.

10   그는 주말에 커피숍에서 일한다. (work)

    → He _____ at a coffee shop on weekends.

11   Sarah는 매일 아침 신문을 읽는다. (read)

    → Sarah _____ the newspaper every morning.

12   Anna는 그녀의 할머니에게 편지를 쓴다. (write)

    → Anna _____ a letter to her grandmother.

B 다음 우리말에 맞도록 괄호 안의 단어를 이용하여 빈칸에 알맞은 말을 쓰시오. (필요시 어형을 바꿀 것)

1 그는 창문을 연다. (open)

→ He _____ the window.

2 그녀는 저녁에 TV를 본다. (watch)

→ She _____ TV in the evening.

3 예지는 나와 함께 영어를 공부한다. (study)

→ Yeji _____ English with me.

4 그녀는 새해에 행운을 기원한다. (wish)

→ She _____ for good luck in the New Year.

5 그는 그 문을 살살 닫는다. (close)

→ He _____ the door gently.

6 그녀는 여름에 우산을 들고 다닌다. (carry)

→ She _____ an umbrella in the summer.

7 그 소년은 그 나무 뒤에 숨는다. (hide)

→ The boy _____ behind the tree.

8 그녀는 재미있는 농담에 웃는다. (laugh)

→ She _____ at funny jokes.

9 민호는 그 시험에 최선을 다한다. (try)

→ Minho _____ his best on the exam.

10 그녀는 매년 여름에 도쿄로 비행기를 타고 간다. (fly)

→ She _____ to Tokyo every summer.

11 새학기는 3월에 시작한다. (begin)

→ The new semester _____ in March.

12 그녀는 토요일마다 도서관에 간다. (go)

→ She _____ to the library on Saturdays.

C **다음 문장을 부정문으로 바꿔 쓰시오.**

1   I eat breakfast every morning.

    → _____

2   She drinks milk every morning.

    → _____

3   I watch TV before bed.

    → _____

4   He runs fast in the race.

    → _____

5   You play the guitar very well.

    → _____

6   He reads the newspaper daily.

    → _____

7   You call your friend.

    → _____

8   He checks his car every two months.

    → _____

9   She teaches English at school.

    → _____

10 It flies over the city.

    → _____

11 We read books at the library.

    → _____

12 It snows a lot in the winter.

    → _____

13 We go to the theater on weekends.

    → _____

14 They study together after school.

    → _____

15 You write a diary every night.

    → _____

D 다음 문장을 의문문으로 바꿔 쓰시오.

1 You drink coffee every morning.

   → _____

2 He wears a hat on sunny days.

   → _____

3 You wait for the bus.

   → _____

4 She exercises at the gym.

   → _____

5 They play soccer on the field.

   → _____

6 It barks loudly at me.

   → _____

7 You walk to school every day.

   → _____

8 They drive to work together.

   → _____

9 She closes the door carefully.

   → _____

10 The students learn new things every day.

   → _____

11 He sleeps early on weekdays.

   → _____

12 The lion lives in the jungle.

   → _____

13 The wind blows softly.

   → _____

14 She buys clothes at the store.

   → _____

15 They swim in the lake.

   → _____

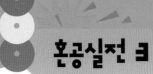

혼공실전 3

1 다음 중 동사의 3인칭 단수 형태가 잘못 짝지어진 것은?

① try – tries

② enjoy – enjoys

③ watch – watches

④ study – studys

⑤ finish – finishes

2 다음 중 밑줄 친 부분이 어법상 틀린 것은?

① We <u>play</u> soccer.

② He <u>write</u> a book.

③ They <u>sing</u> well.

④ I <u>run</u> every morning.

⑤ She <u>eats</u> breakfast.

3 다음 중 빈칸에 들어갈 말로 적절하지 <u>않은</u> 것은?

_____ go to school on foot.

① I   ② We

③ Tom   ④ They

⑤ You and I

4 다음 중 don't가 들어갈 위치로 적절한 것은?

① We ② teach ③ English ④
very well ⑤.

①   ②   ③   ④   ⑤

5 다음 우리말에 맞도록 빈칸에 알맞은 <u>한 단어</u>를 쓰시오.

Sarah는 춤을 아주 잘 추지는 못한다.

→ Sarah _____ dance very well.

6 다음 우리말에 맞도록 빈칸에 알맞은 말을 쓰시오.

그녀는 매일 피아노를 연습하니?

→ _____ she practice the piano
every day?

7 다음 빈칸 (A)와 (B)에 들어갈 말이 바르게 짝지어진 것은?

- I __(A)__ play soccer.
- She __(B)__ sing on the stage.

	(A)		(B)
①	is not	-	is not
②	don't	-	don't
③	don't	-	doesn't
④	doesn't	-	don't
⑤	doesn't	-	doesn't

8 다음 중 밑줄 친 부분이 어법상 **틀린** 것은?

① He <u>talks</u> on the phone.

② We <u>listens</u> to music.

③ The babies <u>like</u> the toy.

④ I <u>help</u> my parents every day.

⑤ She <u>paints</u> pictures on weekends.

9 다음 문장에서 어법상 **틀린** 곳을 찾아 바르게 고치시오.

The sun shine brightly in the sky.

_____ → _____

10 다음 밑줄 친 부분을 부정하여 문장을 다시 쓰시오.

He <u>visits</u> my grandmother on Mondays.

→ _____

11 다음 우리말에 맞도록 빈칸에 알맞은 말을 쓰시오.

그들은 나의 도움이 필요할까?

→ _____ they need my help?

12 다음 중 어법상 **틀린** 것은?

① Tom go to school by bus.

② It jumps into the water.

③ She doesn't work here.

④ Do you clean the house every weekend?

⑤ Does he try his best in every game?

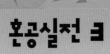

혼공실전 3

[13-15] 다음 우리말에 맞도록 빈칸에 알맞은 말을 보기 에서 골라 쓰시오.

보기 don't   doesn't   do   does

13

아이들은 놀이터에서 놀지 않습니다.

→ The children _____ play in the playground.

14

너는 소풍에 간식을 가져오니?

→ _____ you bring snacks to the picnic?

15

그는 금요일 밤마다 영화를 보지 않는다.

→ He _____ watch movies on Friday nights.

[16-17] 다음 우리말에 맞도록 괄호 안의 단어들을 바르게 배열하시오.

16

너는 매운 음식을 즐기니?
(spicy food / Do / you / enjoy / ?)

→ _____

17

그는 나를 위해 저녁을 요리하지 않는다.
(doesn't / dinner / me / cook / He / for / .)

→ _____

18 다음 문장을 의문문으로 바꿔 쓰시오.

They go to the library on Sundays.

→ _____

[19-20] 다음 대화에서 어법상 **틀린** 곳을 찾아 바르게 고치시오.

19

A: Does she carry a heavy bag?
B: No, she does. Her bag is light.

_____ → _____

20

A: Do they sell fresh fruits?

B: Yes, they don't. I buy some once a week.

_____ → _____

21 다음 질문에 대한 대답으로 가장 적절한 것은?

A: Does he ride his bike every day?

B: _____

① Yes, he do.

② No, he don't.

③ Yes, he doesn't.

④ No, he does.

⑤ Yes, he does.

22 다음 두 대화의 빈칸에 들어갈 말이 바르게 짝지어진 것은?

• A: _____ you like your friends?

  B: Yes, I do.

• A: Does he go shopping after work?

  B: No, he _____.

① Do - does

② Does - does

③ Do - doesn't

④ Does - don't

⑤ Do - do

23 다음 글의 밑줄 친 부분 중 어법상 틀린 곳은?

Emily ①loves to bake. She ②mixes flour, sugar, and eggs every day. Her brother, Tom ③studies in his room. He ④have an exam on Monday. After baking, Emily ⑤shares the cookies with him.

①   ②   ③   ④   ⑤

시제 1
(과거형)

일반동사의 과거형

	규칙	예시
대부분의 동사	동사원형 + ed	play → played
e로 끝나는 동사	동사원형 + d	like → liked
'자음+y'로 끝나는 동사	y를 i로 고치고 + ed	cry → cried
'자음+모음+자음'으로 끝나는 동사	마지막 자음을 한 번 더 쓰고 + ed	stop → stopped

A 다음 괄호 안에서 알맞은 것을 고르시오.

1 The car (stoped / stopped) in front of me.

2 The baby (cries / cried) last night.

3 He (watches / watched) TV yesterday.

4 She (likes / liked) the doll in her childhood.

불규칙 동사 변화

원형	과거형	과거분사형	원형	과거형	과거분사형
go 가다	went	gone	say 말하다	said	said
eat 먹다	ate	eaten	leave 떠나다	left	left
drink 마시다	drank	drunk	keep 유지하다, 지키다	kept	kept
sing 노래하다	sang	sung	buy 사다	bought	bought
do 하다	did	done	hear 듣다	heard	heard
break 깨다, 부수다	broke	broken	read 읽다	read	read
drive 운전하다	drove	driven	bring 가져오다	brought	brought
give 주다	gave	given	build 짓다	built	built
write 쓰다	wrote	written	find 찾다	found	found
see 보다	saw	seen	teach 가르치다	taught	taught
begin 시작하다	began	begun	make 만들다	made	made
run 달리다	ran	run	meet 만나다	met	met
know 알다	knew	known	put 놓다	put	put
take 타다, (사진을) 찍다	took	taken	cut 자르다	cut	cut
fly 날다	flew	flown	hurt 다치게 하다	hurt	hurt

* '과거분사' 내용은 LEVEL 2 '수동태의 시제'에서 자세히 다룹니다.

일반동사 과거형의 부정문

수	인칭	주어	부정문	줄임말
단수	1인칭	I	주어 + did not + 동사원형 ~.	주어 + didn't + 동사원형 ~.
단수	2인칭	You		
단수	3인칭	He, She, It		
복수	1인칭	We		
복수	2인칭	You		
복수	3인칭	They		

B 다음 중 옳은 문장에 동그라미 하시오.

1 He don't liked the toy.   ( )

    He did not like the toy.   ( )

2 We did not play soccer yesterday. ( )

    We didn't played soccer yesterday. ( )

3 They did not sang together last week. ( )

    They didn't sing together last week. ( )

일반동사 과거형의 의문문

수	인칭	주어	의문문	긍정 대답	부정 대답
단수	1인칭	I	Did + 주어 + 동사원형 ~?	Yes, + 주어 + did.	No, + 주어 + didn't.
단수	2인칭	You			
단수	3인칭	He, She, It			
복수	1인칭	We			
복수	2인칭	You			
복수	3인칭	They			

C 다음 대화의 괄호 안에서 알맞은 것을 고르시오.

1 A: (Does / Did) he go to school yesterday?

    B: Yes, he (does / did).

2 A: (Do / Did) they sing together last night?

    B: No, they (did / didn't).

혼공연습

A 다음 괄호 안에서 알맞은 것을 고르시오.

1 I (play / played) soccer an hour ago.

2 He (drinks / drank) coffee this morning.

3 They (eat / ate) breakfast now.

4 They (eat / ate) pie yesterday morning.

5 She (watch / watched) TV yesterday evening.

6 He (go / went) to school by car an hour ago.

7 We (buy / bought) groceries last Monday.

8 They (work / worked) at the office last week.

B 다음 동사를 과거형으로 바꿔 쓰시오.

1	work	→ _____	2	play	→ _____
3	talk	→ _____	4	wash	→ _____
5	start	→ _____	6	love	→ _____
7	move	→ _____	8	live	→ _____
9	close	→ _____	10	hope	→ _____
11	cry	→ _____	12	try	→ _____
13	marry	→ _____	14	carry	→ _____
15	study	→ _____	16	worry	→ _____
17	stop	→ _____	18	plan	→ _____
19	drop	→ _____	20	grab	→ _____

C 다음 문장의 밑줄 친 부분을 과거형으로 바꿔 쓰시오.

1 He <u>likes</u> the book in his childhood.　　　→ _____

2 She <u>studies</u> English yesterday.　　　　　→ _____

3 We <u>visit</u> our uncle last month.　　　　　→ _____

4 I <u>cook</u> dinner last night.　　　　　　　　→ _____

5 She <u>takes</u> a shower before bed yesterday.　→ _____

6 James <u>knows</u> the answer to the question.　→ _____

D 다음 문장을 괄호 안의 지시에 따라 바꿔 쓰시오.

1 We listened to music in the car. (부정문으로)

　　→ _____

2 She learned new words last night. (의문문으로)

　　→ _____

3 They cleaned the house last weekend. (부정문으로)

　　→ _____

4 I opened the window today. (부정문으로)

　　→ _____

5 You jumped rope yesterday. (의문문으로)

　　→ _____

6 We found the wrong answer. (의문문으로)

　　→ _____

A 다음 괄호 안에서 알맞은 것을 고르시오.

1   I (play / played) baseball yesterday.

2   She (watches / watched) a movie last month.

3   They (enter / entered) the museum a few minutes ago.

4   She (climbs / climbed) trees yesterday afternoon.

5   We (walk / walked) in the park this morning.

6   They (share / shared) their snacks two days ago.

7   He (listens / listened) to loud music yesterday.

8   They (greet / greeted) everyone a while ago.

9   We (laugh / laughed) a lot last evening.

10   They (shout / shouted) loudly this afternoon.

11   She (asks / asked) a question this morning.

12   He (starts / started) a new job last week.

13   They (finish / finished) the project last month.

14   He (fixes / fixed) his bike a few days ago.

15   We (visit / visited) our grandparents last summer.

16   They (travel / traveled) to Japan in 2024.

17   She (met / meets) her cousins last winter.

18   He (works / worked) at a café last Monday.

19   They (hike / hiked) up the mountain last fall.

20   They (enjoy / enjoyed) the fireworks last night.

다음 괄호 안에서 알맞은 것을 고르시오.

1   I (goed / went) to the zoo last Sunday.

2   She (broke / breaked) her phone last month.

3   He (drove / drived) to the countryside yesterday.

4   They (ate / eated) pizza for dinner last night.

5   We (see / saw) shooting stars a few nights ago.

6   I (took / taked) a lot of photos during the trip.

7   She (finds / found) her keys last Friday.

8   He (ran / runned) in the park early this morning.

9   They (gave / gived) me a gift on my birthday.

10   We (sing / sang) together at the party last week.

11   I (write / wrote) a letter two days ago.

12   She (bringed / brought) a dog again yesterday.

13   He (buyed / bought) a new computer last summer.

14   They (knew / knowed) the name of their mom's friend.

15   We (began / begin) our homework last night.

16   I (drank / drinked) hot chocolate this morning.

17   She (flyed / flew) to Paris last winter.

18   He (read / reads) an interesting book a few weeks ago.

19   They (keep / kept) their promise last year.

20   I (hear / heard) thunder last night.

혼공실전 1

C 다음 괄호 안에서 알맞은 것을 고르시오.

1 They (didn't sing / didn't sang) a song.

2 He (didn't start / doesn't started) his piano lesson.

3 She (didn't change / didn't changed) her job.

4 He (not joined / did not join) the chess club.

5 She (didn't move / didn't moved) to a new city.

6 I (don't swam / didn't swim) in the sea.

7 She (not planned / did not plan) a trip.

8 He (didn't lose / doesn't lost) his backpack.

9 I (ate not / didn't eat) breakfast this morning.

10 She (didn't write / didn't wrote) an email.

D 다음 중 옳은 문장에 동그라미 하시오.

1 Do you see a rainbow last spring? (   )
   Did you see a rainbow last spring? (   )

2 Do they took the bus last night? (   )
   Did they take the bus last night? (   )

3 Did you read the news this morning? (   )
   Do you read the news this morning? (   )

4 Did she met him a long time ago? (   )
   Did she meet him a long time ago? (   )

5 Did he leave home early this morning? (   )
   Does he left home early this morning? (   )

6 Does your father built this treehouse? (   )
   Did your father build this treehouse? (   )

다음 대화의 괄호 안에서 알맞은 것을 고르시오.

1 A: (Do / Did) you learn Spanish last year?

B: Yes, I (do / did).

2 A: (Did / Does) he visit the dentist last month?

B: No, he (didn't / doesn't).

3 A: Did they (watch / watched) a concert last month?

B: Yes, they (did / does).

4 A: (Did / Does) she watch the movie already?

B: No, she (did / didn't).

5 A: Did you (travel / traveled) to France last year?

B: Yes, I (did / didn't).

6 A: (Did / Does) she start a new business last year?

B: No, she (did / didn't).

7 A: (Do / Did) they learn to cook a long time ago?

B: Yes, they (do / did).

8 A: (Do / Did) you borrow a book last week?

B: No, I (don't / didn't).

9 A: (Do / Did) he water the plants yesterday?

B: Yes, he (did / does).

10 A: (Did / Does) she send a letter a few days ago?

B: Yes, she (did / does).

A 다음 우리말에 맞도록 괄호 안의 단어를 이용하여 빈칸에 알맞은 말을 쓰시오.

1 우리는 어제 저녁에 TV를 봤다. (watch)

→ We _____ TV last evening.

2 그는 체육관에서 농구를 했다. (play)

→ He _____ basketball in the gym.

3 그녀는 친구들과 등산을 했다. (hike)

→ She _____ with her friends.

4 나는 어제 학교에 걸어갔다. (walk)

→ I _____ to school yesterday.

5 그녀는 오늘 아침에 책을 읽었다. (read)

→ She _____ a book this morning.

6 그는 오늘 아침에 차를 타고 출근했다. (drive)

→ He _____ to work this morning.

7 그 고양이가 내 컵을 깨뜨렸다. (break)

→ The cat _____ my cup.

8 그들은 지난 일요일에 함께 점심을 먹었다. (eat)

→ They _____ lunch together last Sunday.

9 나는 어머니에게 편지를 썼다. (write)

→ I _____ a letter to my mother.

10 Jane은 파티에 선물을 가져왔다. (bring)

→ Jane _____ a gift to the party.

11 그녀는 어제 학생들에게 수학을 가르쳤다. (teach)

→ She _____ math to the students yesterday.

12 그들은 오늘 아침에 오렌지 주스를 마셨다. (drink)

→ They _____ orange juice this morning.

B 다음 우리말에 맞도록 빈칸에 알맞은 <u>한 단어</u>를 쓰시오.

1 나는 그 창문을 열었다.

→ I _____ the window.

2 그녀는 어젯밤에 영화를 봤다.

→ She _____ a movie last night.

3 나는 어제 컴퓨터 게임을 하지 않았다.

→ I _____ play computer games yesterday.

4 그는 오늘 아침에 그의 엄마를 도와드리지 않았다.

→ He _____ help his mom this morning.

5 우리는 지난 주말에 동물원을 방문하지 않았다.

→ We _____ visit a zoo last weekend.

6 그는 어제 오후에 그림을 그리지 않았다.

→ He _____ paint a picture yesterday afternoon.

7 너는 네 방을 청소했니?

→ _____ you clean your room?

8 너희 어머니께서 어제 저녁에 파스타를 요리하셨니?

→ _____ your mother cook pasta last evening?

9 지난 토요일에 파티에서 진희가 노래했니?

→ _____ Jinhee sing at the party last Saturday?

10 너는 수업 끝나고 선생님께 갔니?

→ _____ you go to your teacher after class?

11 그녀가 해변에서 모래성을 만들었니?

→ _____ she build a sandcastle at the beach?

12 나는 어젯밤에 그 이상한 소리를 듣지 못했다.

→ I _____ hear the strange noise last night.

C 다음 문장을 부정문으로 바꿔 쓰시오.

1   We talked about the plan.

→ _____

2   He studied English last semester.

→ _____

3   They washed their car.

→ _____

4   We started a new hobby.

→ _____

5   She played the piano.

→ _____

6   They opened a restaurant.

→ _____

7   I went to the park yesterday.

→ _____

8   He saw a rainbow this morning.

→ _____

9   We traveled to the mountains last winter.

→ _____

10 I wrote a short story last Sunday.

→ _____

11 We took photos the day before yesterday.

→ _____

12 She ate ice cream last night.

→ _____

13 They laughed at the joke.

→ _____

14 I bought a new book.

→ _____

15 They gave me a present last Christmas.

→ _____

D 다음 문장을 의문문으로 바꿔 쓰시오.

1   She baked a cake last weekend.

→ _____

2   You listened to music last night.

→ _____

3   She changed her job.

→ _____

4   Your sister drank lemonade.

→ _____

5   He broke his phone.

→ _____

6   He started his guitar lessons.

→ _____

7   She wrote an essay yesterday.

→ _____

8   They swam in the pool.

→ _____

9   Minsu met new friends last week.

→ _____

10 You heard a legend.

→ _____

11 She read an article last weekend.

→ _____

12 He ran in the race.

→ _____

13 Thomas went to the store yesterday.

→ _____

14 They kept the secret.

→ _____

15 She left her bag at school.

→ _____

혼공실전 3

[1–2] **다음 중 동사의 과거형이 잘못 짝지어진 것을 고르시오.**

1

① try - tried

② stop - stopped

③ watch - watched

④ study - studyed

⑤ finish - finished

2

① make - made

② know - knew

③ keep - kept

④ write - wrote

⑤ leave - leaved

[3–4] **다음 중 빈칸에 들어갈 말로 가장 적절한 것을 고르시오.**

We _____ hiking last weekend.

① go

② goed

③ goes

④ went

⑤ going

4

He _____ to India last year.

① fly

② flies

③ flew

④ flyed

⑤ flys

5 **다음 중 did not이 들어갈 위치로 알맞은 것은?**

① He ② leave ③ home ④ early ⑤ yesterday.

①   ②   ③   ④   ⑤

[6–7] **다음 중 밑줄 친 부분이 어법상 틀린 것을 고르시오.**

① She <u>walked</u> to school yesterday.

② He <u>writed</u> a letter to his friend last night.

③ We <u>played</u> soccer in the park last weekend.

④ They <u>helped</u> their parents at the store.

⑤ I <u>cooked</u> dinner for my family last night.

7

① She <u>watched</u> TV last night.

② I <u>sang</u> a song yesterday.

③ He <u>runned</u> in the park this morning.

④ We <u>danced</u> at the party last weekend.

⑤ They <u>talked</u> on the phone two days ago.

8 다음 중 밑줄 친 부분이 어법상 옳은 것은?

① She <u>cryed</u> after the show.

② We <u>didn't went</u> to the zoo last weekend.

③ They <u>buyed</u> new shoes yesterday.

④ He <u>didn't start</u> a new book.

⑤ I <u>readed</u> a novel two days ago.

9 다음 괄호 안의 주어진 단어 중 알맞은 형태를 골라 문장을 다시 쓰시오.

The cat (grab / grabed / grabbed) the mouse yesterday.

→ _____

10 다음 문장에서 어법상 <u>틀린</u> 곳을 찾아 바르게 고치시오.

They didn't walked by the river yesterday.

_____ → _____

[11-13] 다음 우리말에 맞도록 빈칸에 알맞은 말을 보기 에서 골라 쓰시오.

보기

reads   read   drinks   drank   took   takes

11

그녀는 그 책을 읽었다.

→ She _____ the book.

12

그는 매일 아침 커피를 마신다.

→ He _____ coffee every morning.

13

내 아들은 어제 샤워를 했다.

→ My son _____ a shower yesterday.

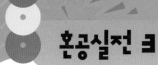

혼공실전 3

[14-15] 다음 우리말에 맞도록 괄호 안의 단어들을 바르게 배열하시오. (필요시 어형을 바꿀 것)

14

나는 지난 주말에 일출을 보았다.
(the sunrise / I / see / last / weekend / .)

→ _____

15

우리는 오늘 아침 공원에서 뛰었다.
(run / we / in the park / this morning / .)

→ _____

[16-17] 다음 대화에서 어법상 <u>틀린</u> 곳을 찾아 바르게 고치시오.

16

A: Did she call you yesterday?
B: Yes, she does.

_____ → _____

17

A: Did you bought it?
B: Yes, I did.

_____ → _____

[18-19] 다음 문장을 의문문으로 바꿔 쓰시오.

18 His friends enjoyed the movie.

→ _____

19 They took the bus to school.

→ _____

20 다음 질문에 대한 대답으로 가장 적절한 것은?

A: Did they wear new clothes on
   Christmas?
B: _____

① Yes, they are.

② No, they don't.

③ Yes, they didn't.

④ No, they didn't.

⑤ Yes, we did.

21 다음 두 대화의 빈칸에 들어갈 말이 바르게 짝지어진 것은?

- A: Did your dog like the food?
  B: No, it _____ .
- A: Did she dance at the concert?
  B: Yes, she _____.

① doesn't – does

② did – did

③ didn't – did

④ didn't – didn't

⑤ doesn't – did

22 다음 글의 밑줄 친 부분 중 어법상 틀린 곳은?

Yesterday, Emily ①lost her house key. She ②looked everywhere. First, she ③searched her bag, but it wasn't there. Then, she ④checks the kitchen, and she went to the living room. She asked her brother, but he ⑤didn't see it.

①   ②   ③   ④   ⑤

23 다음 대화에서 어법상 틀린 곳을 찾아 바르게 고치시오.

A: Did you see the new store?
B: Yes, I did.
A: Did you went inside?
B: No, I didn't.
A: Oh, really? I bought a jacket there.
B: Was the store big?
A: Yes, it was.

_____ → _____

4

시제 2
(미래형과 진행형)

- 미래를 나타내는 will과 be going to
- 동사 + ing 형태
- 현재진행형과 과거진행형
- 진행형의 부정문과 의문문

미래를 나타내는 will과 be going to

	will + 동사원형	be going to + 동사원형
결정 시점	즉석에서 결정한 일	이미 결정된 일
미래 예측 근거	개인의 의견이나 직감에 근거 It will snow next week.	현재의 증거나 상황에 근거 Look! It's going to snow soon.
의지 / 계획	의지를 표현 I will call you later.	계획된 행동이나 의도를 표현 I am going to call my friend tomorrow.
의문문	Will + 주어 + 동사원형 ~?	Be동사 + 주어 + going to + 동사원형 ~?

A 다음 괄호 안에서 알맞은 것을 고르시오.

1 I think it will (rain / rains) next week.

2 Look at those clouds. It is going to (rain / raining).

3 Are you (go / going) to call your friend?

동사 + ing 형태

	규칙	예시
기본 규칙	동사원형 + -ing	read → reading
-e로 끝나는 동사	-e를 없애고 + -ing	make → making
자음 + 모음 + 자음으로 끝나는 동사	마지막 자음을 한 번 더 쓰고 + -ing	run → running
-ie로 끝나는 동사	ie를 y로 바꾸고 + -ing	lie → lying
모음 + y로 끝나는 동사	y를 그대로 두고 + -ing	play → playing
예외 동사	일부 동사는 e로 끝나도 그대로 + -ing -ee로 끝나는 동사는 그대로 + -ing	be → being, see → seeing

B 다음 동사를 -ing 형태로 바꿔 쓰시오.

1 watch → _____

2 come → _____

3 sit → _____

4 die → _____

5 play → _____

	규칙		예문
현재진행형 am / are / is + -ing	I am You are He / She / It is We are You are They are	+ -ing	I am running. You are running. He / She / It is running. We are running. You are running. They are running.
과거진행형 was / were + -ing	I was You were He / She / It was We were You were They were	+ -ing	I was running. You were running. He / She / It was running. We were running. You were running. They were running.

C 다음 중 옳은 문장에 동그라미 하시오.

1 He is sing now.   (   )

   He is singing now.   (   )

2 They watching TV.   (   )

   They were watching TV.   (   )

	현재진행형	과거진행형
긍정문	주어 + be동사 + -ing She is reading a book.	주어 + be동사의 과거형 + -ing She was reading a book.
부정문	주어 + be동사 + not + -ing She is not reading a book.	주어 + be동사의 과거형 + not + -ing She was not reading a book.
부정문 축약형	'm not / aren't / isn't + -ing She isn't reading a book.	wasn't / weren't + -ing She wasn't reading a book.
의문문	Be동사 + 주어 + -ing ~? Is she reading a book?	Be동사의 과거형 + 주어 + -ing ~? Was she reading a book?

D 다음 대화의 괄호 안에서 알맞은 것을 고르시오.

1 A: (Am / Are) you reading a book?

   B: Yes, I (am / are).

2 A: (Was / Were) you singing with him?

   B: No, I (wasn't / didn't).

A 다음 괄호 안에서 알맞은 것을 고르시오.

1 I will (call / calling) you tomorrow.

2 They will (arrive / arrives) at 6 p.m.

3 She will (bake / bakes) a cake for the party.

4 Will you (open / opening) the window?

5 They are (go / going) to travel this summer.

6 He is going to (start / starts) a new job next month.

7 (Are / Will) you going to watch the soccer game?

8 She is going to (take / taking) piano lessons.

B 다음 동사를 알맞은 형태로 바꿔 쓰시오.

		현재진행	과거진행
1	walk	is walking	was walking
2	talk		
3	finish		
4	circle		
5	eat		
6	hunt		
7	run		
8	play		
9	sit		
10	read		

C 다음 문장을 괄호 안의 지시에 따라 바꿔 쓰시오.

1 I read a book. (현재진행형으로)

   → _____

2 She cooks dinner. (현재진행형으로)

   → _____

3 They play soccer. (현재진행형으로)

   → _____

4 I run in the morning. (과거진행형으로)

   → _____

5 She sings a beautiful song. (과거진행형으로)

   → _____

6 We wait for the bus. (과거진행형으로)

   → _____

D 다음 문장을 괄호 안의 지시에 따라 바꿔 쓰시오.

1 We are watching a movie. (부정문으로)

   → _____

2 The baby is crying loudly. (부정문으로)

   → _____

3 My father was fixing his bike. (의문문으로)

   → _____

4 Your sister was reading a book. (의문문으로)

   → _____

5 She was not cooking dinner. (축약형으로)

   → _____

6 He is not studying for his exam. (축약형으로)

   → _____

A 다음 괄호 안에서 알맞은 것을 고르시오.

1   It will (rain / rains) tomorrow.

2   He will (buy / bought) a new car next month.

3   She will (invite / invites) her friends to her house.

4   They will (watch / watched) the concert tonight.

5   I will (call / calling) the doctor tomorrow.

6   We will (clean / cleaning) the house this afternoon.

7   He will (bring / bringing) his guitar to the picnic.

8   They are (go / going) to build a new school in this area.

9   We are going to (move / moving) to a new house soon.

10   He (is / will) going to lead a new club this weekend.

11   I am going to (bake / bakes) cookies this afternoon.

12   She is going to (buy / buys) a computer tomorrow.

13   We (are / is) going to meet at the café at 4 p.m.

14   He is going to (run / running) a marathon next month.

15   I am going to (read / reading) that book tonight.

16   (Is / Will) she going to attend the workshop?

17   (Are / Will) you join us for dinner?

18   Will they (come / coming) to the concert?

19   Will you (help / helping) me with this project?

20   Are they (go / going) to visit us during the holidays?

B 다음 괄호 안에서 알맞은 것을 고르시오.

1   I am (walking / walkking) to school.

2   They are (comeing / coming) to the party.

3   She is (swiming / swimming) in the pool.

4   He is (siting / sitting) on the bench.

5   I am (stoping / stopping) the car.

6   They are (runing / running) in the race.

7   She is (lying / lieing) on the bed.

8   She is (talkking / talking) to her friend.

9   He is (jumping / jumpping) on the trampoline.

10   They are (playing / playying) soccer.

11   She is (making / makeing) a cake.

12   He is (writing / writting) a letter.

13   I am (taking / takeing) a break.

14   He is (cuting / cutting) his hair.

15   They are (trying / tryying) a new recipe.

16   We are (applying / appling) for a job.

17   She is (enjoing / enjoying) the concert.

18   He is (practicing / practiceing) the guitar.

19   I am (buying / buyying) groceries.

20   He is (seing / seeing) the doctor now.

C 다음 괄호 안에서 알맞은 것을 고르시오.

1 They (are / were) walking on the street now.

2 He (is / was) cleaning the windows yesterday afternoon.

3 I (am / was) listening to music now.

4 She (is / was) drinking coffee thirty minutes ago.

5 He (is / was) playing a board game at 1 p.m. yesterday.

6 The kids (are / were) laughing at me right now.

7 We (are / were) waiting for the train now.

8 He (is / was) fixing his laptop right now.

9 The baby (is / was) crying loudly early this morning.

10 She (is / was) writing a letter last night.

11 He (is / was) swimming in the pool yesterday afternoon.

12 They (are / were) talking in the café yesterday evening.

13 I (am / was) riding a bicycle last night.

14 She (is / was) drinking coffee yesterday morning.

15 She (is / was) writing a letter right now.

16 He (is / was) painting one hour ago.

17 She (is / was) singing at the concert right now.

18 They (are / were) playing soccer yesterday afternoon.

19 He (is / was) studying for his exam yesterday night.

20 We (are / were) watching a movie last weekend.

D 다음 대화의 괄호 안에서 알맞은 것을 고르시오.

1 A: (Is / Are) she listening to music?
   B: Yes, she (is / are).

2 A: (Am / Are) they playing basketball?
   B: No, they (isn't / aren't).

3 A: (Was / Were) she reading a book last night?
   B: Yes, she (was / were).

4 A: (Was / Were) they playing video games yesterday afternoon?
   B: No, they (wasn't / weren't).

5 A: (Was / Were) you writing an email at 9 p.m. yesterday?
   B: Yes, I (was / were).

6 A: (Is / Are) he watching TV?
   B: Yes, he (is / are).

7 A: (Am / Are) you studying for the test?
   B: No, I (am / am not).

8 A: (Was / Were) he sleeping at that time?
   B: No, he (wasn't / weren't).

9 A: (Is / Are) it raining outside?
   B: No, it (isn't / aren't).

A 다음 우리말에 맞도록 빈칸에 알맞은 단어를 쓰시오.

1 나는 다음 주에 시험공부를 할 것이다.

→ I _____ study for the test next week.

2 우리는 곧 숙제를 할 예정이다.

→ We _____ _____ to do homework soon.

3 그가 내일 새로운 것을 시도할 예정인가요?

→ _____ he _____ to try something new tomorrow?

4 그는 내일 그 공원에 갈 예정이다.

→ He _____ _____ to go to the park tomorrow.

5 우리는 곧 저녁을 먹을 것이다.

→ We _____ have dinner soon.

6 그녀는 새 책을 읽을 예정이다.

→ She _____ _____ to read a new book.

7 그들은 오늘 저녁 식사를 할 건가요?

→ _____ they eat dinner tonight?

8 당신은 다음 주에 여행을 갈 예정인가요?

→ _____ you _____ to go on a trip next week?

9 그녀는 내일 그 수업에 참여할 예정인가요?

→ _____ she _____ to attend the class tomorrow?

10 그들은 한 시간 후에 역에 도착할 것이다.

→ They _____ arrive at the station in an hour.

11 그들은 오늘 밤 영화를 볼 예정이다.

→ They _____ _____ to watch a movie tonight.

12 그는 다음 달에 새로운 일을 시작할 예정인가요?

→ _____ he _____ to start a new job next month?

B 다음 우리말에 맞도록 괄호 안의 단어를 이용하여 빈칸에 알맞은 단어를 쓰시오.

1 그녀는 피아노를 치고 있다. (play)

→ She is _____ the piano.

2 그들은 축구공을 차고 있다. (kick)

→ They are _____ the soccer ball.

3 나는 그림을 그리고 있다. (draw)

→ I am _____ a picture.

4 그는 지금 자고 있다. (sleep)

→ He is _____ now.

5 우리는 수영장에서 수영하고 있다. (swim)

→ We are _____ in the pool.

6 그녀는 무대에서 춤을 추고 있다. (dance)

→ She is _____ on the stage.

7 나는 편지를 쓰고 있다. (write)

→ I am _____ a letter.

8 그들은 새로운 단어들을 배우고 있다. (learn)

→ They are _____ new words.

9 우리는 비행기를 기다리고 있다. (wait)

→ We are _____ for the plane.

10 나의 엄마는 쿠키를 만들고 있다. (make)

→ My mom is _____ cookies.

11 그 고양이가 소파에 누워 있다. (lie)

→ The cat is _____ on the sofa.

12 그들은 콘서트를 즐기고 있다. (enjoy)

→ They are _____ the concert.

C 다음 문장을 괄호 안의 지시에 따라 바꿔 쓰시오.

1 I have a good time. (현재진행형으로)

→ _____

2 We enjoy good weather. (현재진행형으로)

→ _____

3 He gives her a gift. (현재진행형으로)

→ _____

4 She smiles for the photo. (현재진행형으로)

→ _____

5 They use the computer. (현재진행형으로)

→ _____

6 They stay at a hotel. (현재진행형으로)

→ _____

7 We played at the park. (과거진행형으로)

→ _____

8 She painted the walls. (과거진행형으로)

→ _____

9 I brushed my teeth. (과거진행형으로)

→ _____

10 They planted flowers in the garden. (과거진행형으로)

→ _____

11 She washed her hands. (과거진행형으로)

→ _____

12 We are carrying heavy bags. (부정문으로)

→ _____

13 She is studying in the library. (부정문으로)

→ _____

14 They were shopping at the mall. (부정문으로)

→ _____

15 He was talking on the phone. (부정문으로)

→ _____

D 다음 문장을 의문문으로 바꿔 쓰시오.

1 You will finish the report by Monday.

   → _____

2 They will have lunch together next Friday.

   → _____

3 You will study harder for the test.

   → _____

4 She is going to study in Canada next year.

   → _____

5 We are going to have barbecue tomorrow.

   → _____

6 She is sleeping on the sofa.

   → _____

7 He is working on a project.

   → _____

8 Youngjoo is running on the track.

   → _____

9 They are laughing at a clown.

   → _____

10 The dogs are sitting by the lake.

   → _____

11 He was driving to work.

   → _____

12 She was knitting a scarf.

   → _____

13 You were making a dress.

   → _____

14 They were dancing at the party.

   → _____

15 He was reading the newspaper.

   → _____

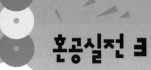

혼공실전 ㅋ

1 다음 중 동사의 -ing 형태가 올바른 것은?

① sit → siting

② see → seing

③ have → haveing

④ write → writting

⑤ agree → agreeing

2 다음 중 동사의 -ing 형태가 **틀린** 것은?

① lie → lying

② fix → fixing

③ die → dieing

④ play → playing

⑤ stop → stopping

3 다음 중 빈칸에 들어갈 말로 가장 적절한 것은?

> We _____ to the wedding this weekend.

① going   ② goes

③ will go   ④ goed

⑤ were going

4 다음 중 밑줄 친 부분이 어법상 **틀린** 것은?

① It will <u>rain</u> next week.

② Will he <u>join</u> the meeting later?

③ I am going to <u>clean</u> my room after lunch.

④ Are you going to <u>calling</u> your friend?

⑤ We are going to <u>paint</u> the living room.

5 다음 중 not이 들어갈 위치로 알맞은 것은?

> They ① are ② studying ③ for ④ the exam ⑤ now.

①   ②   ③   ④   ⑤

6 다음 빈칸에 공통으로 들어갈 말로 적절한 것은?

> • You _____ planning a new schedule.
> • We _____ going to visit your uncle.

① am   ② to

③ will   ④ are

⑤ is

7. 다음 중 밑줄 친 부분이 어법상 **틀린** 것은?

① The kids <u>are playing</u> soccer.

② I <u>is reading</u> a book.

③ We <u>are listening</u> to music.

④ She <u>is taking</u> a shower.

⑤ They <u>are talking</u> on the phone.

8. 다음 중 어법상 **틀린** 문장을 <u>모두</u> 고르면?

① She was walking to school.

② They wasn't watching TV.

③ I was studying in my room.

④ He were eating dinner at 8 p.m.

⑤ We weren't playing badminton in the park.

9. 다음 우리말에 맞도록 빈칸에 알맞은 단어를 쓰시오.

그들은 큰 행사를 개최할 예정이다.

→ They _____ _____
_____ hold a big event.

10. 다음 문장에서 어법상 **틀린** 곳을 찾아 바르게 고치시오.

They were planting flowers in the garden now.

_____ → _____

11. 다음 질문에 대한 대답으로 가장 적절한 것은?

Were they building a sandcastle?

① Yes, we do.

② No, they didn't.

③ Yes, they do.

④ No, we weren't.

⑤ No, they weren't.

12. 다음 우리말에 맞도록 빈칸 (A)와 (B)에 들어갈 말이 바르게 짝지어진 것은?

• 우리는 곧 비행기를 탈 것이다.
  → We __(A)__ take a flight soon.
• 그들은 숨바꼭질을 하는 중이었다.
  → They __(B)__ playing hide-and-seek.

   (A)   (B)

① are   - are

② will   - were

③ going - were

④ going - are

⑤ will   - are

[13-15] 다음 그림에 맞도록 빈칸에 알맞은 말을 보기 에서 골라 현재진행형으로 바꿔 쓰시오.

보기   sleep   talk   play

13

He _____ _____ basketball.

14

He _____ _____ on the bed.

15

They _____ _____ about their friends.

[16-18] 다음 그림에 맞도록 괄호 안의 단어를 이용하여 현재진행형 문장을 완성하시오.

16

A: _____ she _____(eat) a slice of pizza?

B: Yes, she _____.

17

A: _____ she singing a song?

B: No, she _____.
   She is _____(cook).

18

A: _____ you listening to music?

B: No, I _____ _____. I am _____(solve) a math problem.

[19-20] **다음 우리말에 맞도록 괄호 안의 표현들을 바르게 배열하시오. (필요시 어형을 바꿀 것)**

19

우리는 새로운 프로젝트를 시작할 예정이다.
(start / be / to / going / a new project / we / .)

→ _____

20

그녀는 공원에서 조깅을 하고 있었다.
(in / jog / she / the park / be / .)

→ _____

21 다음 대화에서 어법상 <u>틀린</u> 곳을 찾아 바르게 고치시오.

A: Was you and Tom studying
   in the library?
B: Yes, we were.

_____ → _____

[22-23] **다음 글을 읽고 물음에 답하시오.**

It _____ raining outside. Jane was reading a book by the window. Her brother was play video games in the living room. Suddenly, the lights went out. They searched for a flashlight in the dark. Then, the power came back. So Jane and her brother laughed.

22 위 글의 빈칸에 들어갈 말로 가장 적절한 것은?

① will

② is going to

③ are

④ was

⑤ is

23 위 글에서 어법상 <u>틀린</u> 곳을 찾아 바르게 고치시오.

_____ → _____

조동사

조동사의 개념과 형태

조동사	의미	예문 (조동사 + 동사원형)
can	능력, 가능성, 허락	I can swim. (능력) 나는 수영할 수 있다.
may	약한 추측, 허락	It may rain. (약한 추측) 비가 올지도 모른다.
must	의무, 강한 추측	You must finish this. (의무) 당신은 이것을 끝내야 한다.
should	의무, 충고	He should take vitamin C. (의무, 충고) 그는 비타민 C를 섭취해야 한다.
will	의지, 결심, 단순 미래	I will change my mind. (의지, 결심) 나는 내 생각을 바꿀 것이다.

A 다음 괄호 안에서 알맞은 것을 고르시오.

1 He can (dance / dances).

2 You must (start / started) your work now.

3 You may (enter / entering) the room.

조동사의 부정형

조동사	부정형(축약형)	의미	예문
can	cannot (can't)	~할 수 없다	I cannot swim. 나는 수영할 수 없다.
may	may not (축약형 없음)	~하면 안 된다, ~하지 않을지도 모른다	You may not enter. 당신은 들어오면 안 된다.
must	must not (mustn't)	절대 ~해서는 안 된다	You must not cheat. 당신은 절대 부정행위를 해서는 안 된다.
should	should not (shouldn't)	~하면 안 된다	You should not run. 당신은 뛰면 안 된다.
will	will not (won't)	~하지 않을 것이다	I will not go there. 나는 그곳에 가지 않을 것이다.

B 다음 괄호 안에서 알맞은 것을 고르시오.

1 He (must not / not must) lie to his parents.

2 Minji (not will / will not) go on a picnic.

	can	may	will
과거형	could (과거의 능력, 가능성, 정중한 요청)	might (낮은 가능성)	would (의지, 정중한 요청, 과거의 습관)
예문	I could climb the tree last summer. 나는 작년 여름에 그 나무를 오를 수 있었다.	It might rain later. 나중에 비가 올지도 모른다.	He said he would call later. 그는 나중에 전화하겠다고 말했다.
의문문	Can + 주어 + 동사원형 ~?	May + 주어 + 동사원형 ~?	Will + 주어 + 동사원형 ~?

C 다음 문장의 올바른 의문문에 동그라미 하시오.

1 You can teach me. → Do you teach me?　(　)

　　　　　　　　　　　　 Can you teach me?　(　)

2 He may come in.　→ May he do come in? (　)

　　　　　　　　　　　　 May he come in?　　(　)

	must	have to
평서문	You must finish your homework. 너는 숙제를 끝내야 한다.	I have to attend the meeting. 나는 회의에 참석해야 한다.
부정형 예문	must not(mustn't): 절대 ~해서는 안 된다 You must not park here. 너는 절대 이곳에 주차해서는 안 된다.	do not(don't) have to: ~할 필요가 없다 (부정형인 경우 의무가 아님) You don't have to come early. 너는 일찍 올 필요가 없다.
의문문	Must + 주어 + 동사원형 ~?	Do / Does / Did + 주어 + have to + 동사원형 ~?
과거형	없음 (대체 표현: had to)	had to

D 다음 대화의 괄호 안에서 알맞은 것을 고르시오.

A: (Do / Must) I study today?

B: Yes, you (do / must).

A 다음 괄호 안에서 알맞은 것을 각 의미에 맞게 고르시오.

1 You (must / can) wear a helmet. (의무)

2 He (can / will) solve the problem easily. (능력)

3 She (must / may) leave early. (허락)

4 Students (may / must) follow the school rules. (의무)

5 We (must / will) meet at the library tomorrow. (미래)

6 They (may / must) come to the party. (허락)

7 You (will / must) practice the piano every day. (의무)

8 We (must / can) be there by noon. (능력)

B 다음 괄호 안에서 알맞은 것을 고르시오.

1 You can (go / going) to the park after school.

2 She may (visit / visits) her grandmother this weekend.

3 They must (complete / completed) the project by tomorrow.

4 We will (start / starts) the meeting in five minutes.

5 He will (call / calling) you tomorrow evening.

6 You can (drive / driving) after high school.

7 She must (finish / finished) her homework.

8 They will (join / joins) us at the restaurant later.

C 다음 문장을 부정문으로 바꿔 쓰시오.

1 I will call you later.

→ _____

2 You can open the door now.

→ _____

3 She may leave early today.

→ _____

4 We must attend the class tomorrow.

→ _____

5 She must know the answer.

→ _____

6 We have to clean the room today.

→ _____

D 다음 문장을 의문문으로 바꿔 쓰시오.

1 You can drive a car.

→ _____

2 She may join the meeting tomorrow.

→ _____

3 He must write his report today.

→ _____

4 We can meet them at the café.

→ _____

5 We will finish the assignment soon.

→ _____

6 She has to go to the doctor tomorrow.

→ _____

A 다음 괄호 안에서 알맞은 것을 고르시오.

1   He must (prepare / preparing) for his presentation.

2   I will (call / calling) the police later.

3   She can (swim / swims) very fast.

4   You may (leave / leaving) the room after the class.

5   We can (finish / finished) this project by tonight.

6   Students must (wear / wearing) uniforms at school.

7   He may (arrive / arriving) late due to traffic.

8   He will (help / helping) you with your luggage.

9   You must (do / doing) this task before the deadline.

10   He (is / will) going to lead a new club this weekend.

11   She must (lead / leads) the team for this project.

12   It may (rain / rains) this afternoon, so take an umbrella.

13   They must (clean / cleaning) up after the event.

14   We will (meet / meets) at the train station soon.

15   You can (use / uses) my computer for your assignment.

16   He can (complete / completing) his work.

17   She must (follow / to following) the safety rules in the lab.

18   You may (borrow / borrowing) my pen for a moment.

19   She can (play / playing) tennis very well.

20   We will (attend / attending) the wedding ceremony tomorrow.

B 다음 우리말에 맞도록 괄호 안에서 알맞은 것을 고르시오.

1   우리는 지금 떠나야 한다.

→ We (can / must) leave now.

2   나는 피아노를 매우 잘 칠 수 있다.

→ I (can / will) play the piano very well.

3   너는 이제 말해도 된다.

→ You (may / must) speak now.

4   우리는 이 일을 완료해야 한다.

→ We (may / must) complete this work.

5   그녀는 오늘 늦게 올지도 모른다.

→ She (may / will) come late today.

6   우리는 정오에 만날 것이다.

→ We (will / must) meet at noon.

7   내가 널 도와줄 수 있다.

→ I (can / will) help you.

8   그녀는 이 규칙을 따라야 한다.

→ She (can / must) follow this rule.

9   나는 지금 계획을 바꿔야 한다.

→ I (may / must) change the plan now.

10 그는 이 시험을 통과해야 한다.

→ He (can / must) pass this exam.

11 나는 내일 너를 안내할 수 있다.

→ I (can / must) guide you tomorrow.

12 나는 이 문제를 빠르게 풀 것이다.

→ I (can / will) solve this problem quickly.

혼공실전 1

C 다음 괄호 안에서 알맞은 것을 고르시오.

1 They (may not / doesn't may) leave without permission.

2 You (cannot / don't can) finish this project alone.

3 He (will not / doesn't will) leave us without a word.

4 She (may not / don't may) attend the meeting today.

5 We (will not / not will) finish our work by noon.

6 The children (must not / don't must) play near the road.

7 You (cannot / don't can) use your phone during the exam.

8 He (won't / won't not) break the rules of the game.

9 She (may not / doesn't may) borrow my book right now.

10 They (not will / will not) arrive before dinner.

D 다음 밑줄 친 부분을 과거형으로 바꿔 쓰시오. (단, 과거형이 없는 경우 대체 표현을 쓸 것)

1 He <u>can</u> run very fast. → _____

2 You <u>must</u> finish your homework before the deadline. → _____

3 I finally <u>can</u> meet her at the station yesterday. → _____

4 They <u>must</u> get home by 10 o'clock. → _____

5 He <u>can</u> solve difficult problems easily. → _____

6 You <u>must</u> attend the class yesterday. → _____

7 They <u>can</u> inform us about the changes. → _____

8 She <u>has to</u> take this book to school. → _____

9 She <u>can</u> run very fast in elementary school. → _____

10 I <u>have to</u> work late last night. → _____

E 다음 대화의 괄호 안에서 알맞은 것을 고르시오.

1   A: Can you (help / helping) me carry this box?

    B: Yes, I (can / may).

2   A: (Do / May) I leave early today?

    B: Yes, you (may / will), but please finish your work first.

3   A: (Will / Must) I finish the report by 5 p.m.?

    B: No, you (must / don't have to).

4   A: Can we (go / going) to the park this afternoon?

    B: That's a great idea!

5   A: (May / Will) you attend the event tomorrow?

    B: No, I (will / won't).

6   A: Can we (watch / watching) a movie tonight?

    B: Sorry, we (can / can't). We have to finish our homework.

7   A: (May / Must) I borrow your notebook for the class?

    B: Of course, you (may / may not).

8   A: (May / Will) you help me prepare for the test?

    B: Sure, I (will / won't).

9   A: (Can / Will) you fix this computer for me?

    B: Yes, I (can / can't).

A 다음 우리말에 맞도록 빈칸에 알맞은 조동사를 쓰시오.

1 그는 바이올린을 아주 잘 연주할 수 있다.

→ He _____ play the violin very well.

2 우리는 지금 떠나야 한다.

→ We _____ leave now.

3 그녀는 오늘 늦게 올지도 모른다.

→ She _____ come late today.

4 우리는 내일 이 프로젝트를 끝낼 것이다.

→ We _____ finish this project tomorrow.

5 그는 하루 종일 일한 다음이라 분명 피곤할 것이다.

→ He _____ be tired after working all day.

6 그녀는 이 문제를 풀지도 모른다.

→ She _____ solve this problem.

7 우리는 오후에 공원에 갈 것이다.

→ We _____ go to the park in the afternoon.

8 그는 그 규칙들을 반드시 따라야 한다.

→ He _____ follow the rules.

9 비가 올지도 모르니 창문을 닫아라.

→ It _____ rain, so close the window.

10 그 앵무새는 아름답게 노래할 수 있다.

→ The parrot _____ sing beautifully.

11 너는 언제든 돌아와도 된다.

→ You _____ come back anytime.

12 모든 사람은 안전벨트를 착용해야 한다.

→ Everyone _____ wear a seat belt.

B 다음 우리말에 맞도록 빈칸에 알맞은 단어를 보기 에서 골라 쓰시오.

보기   could   had to   would

1   그는 어렸을 때 피아노를 칠 수 있었다.
    → He _____ play the piano in his childhood.

2   우리는 일찍 떠나야 했다.
    → We _____ leave early.

3   그녀는 그 책을 읽을 수 있었다.
    → She _____ read that book.

4   나는 어제 그 보고서를 끝내야만 했다.
    → I _____ finish the report yesterday.

5   그는 다음날 그 회의에 참석해야 했다.
    → He _____ attend the meeting the next day.

6   그는 다음 주에 올 거라고 말했다.
    → He said he _____ come next week.

7   나는 그 노래의 가사를 쉽게 이해할 수 있었다.
    → I _____ understand that song's lyrics easily.

8   우리는 언젠가 다시 만날 것이다.
    → We _____ meet again someday.

9   그녀는 병원에 가야만 했다.
    → She _____ go to the hospital.

10 그녀는 그 퍼즐을 빠르게 풀 수 있었다.
    → She _____ solve the puzzle quickly.

11 그들은 나중에 우리와 저녁식사를 함께 할 것이다.
    → They _____ join us for dinner later.

12 그는 항상 그녀에게 꽃을 가져다주곤 했다.
    → He _____ always bring flowers for her.

C 다음 문장을 부정문으로 바꿔 쓰시오.

1 I can finish this task alone.

→ _____

2 She may use my phone.

→ _____

3 They must be poor.

→ _____

4 They will attend the ceremony tomorrow.

→ _____

5 We must waste time on unnecessary things.

→ _____

6 He could solve the problem yesterday.

→ _____

7 She might come to the party tonight.

→ _____

8 You should skip your breakfast.

→ _____

9 I can understand the instructions clearly.

→ _____

10 You must forget to lock the door.

→ _____

11 They will agree to our plan.

→ _____

12 He could believe the news.

→ _____

13 She might see the email.

→ _____

14 You should speak to others that way.

→ _____

15 He would listen to any advice.

→ _____

D 다음 문장을 의문문으로 바꿔 쓰시오.

1 You can help me.

→ _____

2 I may leave the class early today.

→ _____

3 We must finish all the exercises in the book.

→ _____

4 You will attend the workshop tomorrow.

→ _____

5 You could explain this concept to me.

→ _____

6 You had to complete the task by yesterday.

→ _____

7 I have to apologize to him for the mistake.

→ _____

8 She can play the guitar well.

→ _____

9 We may use the library after hours.

→ _____

10 He must finish the assignment today.

→ _____

11 You will open the window for me.

→ _____

12 They will visit us this Christmas.

→ _____

13 He could solve the problem on his own.

→ _____

14 You had to wake up early yesterday.

→ _____

15 You would like some tea.

→ _____

혼공실전 3

1 다음 중 조동사와 그 의미가 <u>잘못</u> 짝지어진 것은?

① can - 능력, 가능성

② may - 약한 추측, 허락

③ must - 제안, 허락

④ should - 의무, 충고

⑤ will - 의지, 결심

2 다음 중 조동사의 부정 축약형이 <u>틀린</u> 것은?

① cannot → can't

② will not → won't

③ may not → mayn't

④ must not → mustn't

⑤ could not → couldn't

3 다음 중 빈칸에 들어갈 말로 적절하지 <u>않은</u> 것은?

She _____ use the computer.

① will　　② has

③ may　　④ must

⑤ can

4 다음 중 빈칸에 들어갈 말로 가장 적절한 것은?

He will _____ the meeting.

① attends　　② attending

③ to attend　　④ attended

⑤ attend

5 다음 중 not이 들어갈 위치로 알맞은 것은?

We ① may ② go ③ to ④ the park ⑤ today.

①　　②　　③　　④　　⑤

6 다음 우리말에 맞도록 빈칸에 들어갈 말로 가장 적절한 것은?

• 그들은 분명 지금 학교에 있을 것이다.
　→ They _____ be at school now.

① can　　② may

③ will　　④ can't

⑤ must

7 다음 중 밑줄 친 부분이 어법상 **틀린** 것은?

① He <u>can't</u> do his homework.

② They <u>may not</u> leave the class now.

③ We <u>must not</u> talk loudly in the library.

④ She <u>doesn't will</u> attend the event.

⑤ Tom <u>cannot</u> ride a bicycle.

8 다음 중 조동사의 과거형이 **잘못** 짝지어진 것은?

① can - could

② will - would

③ may - might

④ must - musted

⑤ have to - had to

9 다음 문장에서 어법상 **틀린** 곳을 찾아 바르게 고치시오.

She could sings very well in the choir last year.

_____ → _____

10 다음 중 빈칸에 들어갈 말로 가장 적절한 것은?

She _____ play the guitar five years ago.

① will ② can

③ may ④ could

⑤ is going to

11 다음 중 어법상 **틀린** 것은?

① He might be at home now.

② She can speak three languages fluently.

③ You should completed this task by tomorrow.

④ We must wear uniforms at school.

⑤ They could take a break.

12 다음 두 대화의 빈칸에 들어갈 말이 바르게 짝지어진 것은?

A: _____ you solve the math question?
B: No, I _____. It is too difficult.

① Can - can't

② Must - musn't

③ Can - can

④ Must - must

⑤ Should - could

[13-16] 다음 우리말에 맞도록 빈칸에 알맞은 말을 보기 에서 골라 쓰시오. (단, 한 번씩만 쓸 것)

보기 can will may could

13

나중에 너에게 전화할게.

→ I _____ call you later.

14

그들은 식사를 준비할 수 있다.

→ They _____ prepare the meal.

15

너는 질문해도 돼.

→ You _____ ask questions.

16

우리는 어젯밤에 별을 선명하게 볼 수 있었다.

→ We _____ see the stars clearly last night.

17 다음 질문에 대한 대답으로 가장 적절한 것은?

A: Did you have to stay late at school?

B: _____

① Yes, I can.
② No, I don't.
③ Yes, I have to.
④ No, I must stay.
⑤ No, I didn't have to.

[18-19] 다음 대화에서 어법상 <u>틀린</u> 곳을 찾아 바르게 고치시오.

18

A: Do we have to complete the English assignment by tomorrow?
B: No, we not have to.

_____ → _____

19

A: Did you had to ask the teacher for help with the project?
B: Yes, I did.

_____ → _____

20 다음 단어들을 바르게 배열하여 문장을 완성하시오.

to / not / have / worry / does

→ She _____
about the test.

23 다음 글의 밑줄 친 부분 중 어법상 틀린 곳은?

School Rules
Students ①<u>must</u> wear uniforms every day. They ②<u>should</u> arrive on time for classes. They ③<u>may</u> not use mobile phones during lessons. All students ④<u>has</u> to complete their homework on time. They can ⑤<u>ask</u> their teachers questions anytime.

①   ②   ③   ④   ⑤

[21-22] 다음 우리말에 맞도록 괄호 안의 단어들을 바르게 배열하시오.

21
내가 네 책을 빌려도 될까?
(borrow / may / I / your book / ?)

→ _____

22
그들은 분명 서로 모르는 사이가 아닐 것이다.
(be / strangers / they / not / must / .)

→ _____

명사와 관사

명사의 종류

셀 수 있는 명사	관사 a / an 또는 숫자 one, two, three 등을 사용하여 셀 수 있음 복수형으로 사용할 수 있음 예시: apple, car, dog, table, friend, park, tree, store, pencil 등	
셀 수 없는 명사	관사 a / an을 붙일 수 없음 복수형으로 쓸 수 없고 단수 형태만 존재함	
	고유명사	Sam, Korea, Mt. Everest 등
	추상명사	love, peace, happiness 등
	물질명사	water, air, soap, gold, rain, bread, wood, paper, butter 등

A 다음 괄호 안에서 알맞은 것을 고르시오.

1 I have (pencil / a pencil).

2 I saw (dog / a dog) this morning.

3 I drink (water / a water) with my meal.

명사의 규칙 복수형

	규칙	예시
일반적인 경우	명사 + s	cat → cats color → colors
-s, -x, -ch, -sh로 끝나는 경우	명사 + es	bus → buses fox → foxes watch → watches dish → dishes
자음 + o로 끝나는 경우	명사 + es	tomato → tomatoes hero → heroes 예외: pianos, photos, radios
자음 + y로 끝나는 경우	y를 i로 바꾸고 + -es	city → cities lady → ladies
-f, -fe로 끝나는 경우	f, fe를 v로 바꾸고 + -es	leaf → leaves knife → knives

B 다음 명사의 복수형을 쓰시오.

1 pig   → _____

2 class   → _____

3 mango → _____

4 puppy → _____

5 wolf   → _____

명사의 불규칙 복수형

구분	예시
모음이 변하는 경우	man – men foot – feet goose – geese tooth – teeth woman – women mouse – mice
어미가 변하는 경우	child – children ox – oxen
단수와 복수가 같은 경우	deer – deer sheep – sheep fish – fish salmon – salmon

C 다음 명사의 복수형을 쓰시오.

1 woman → _____

2 child → _____

3 ox → _____

4 tooth → _____

5 sheep → _____

관사 a / an, the

부정관사 a / an 특정하지 않은 단수 명사와 사용	자음으로 시작할 때	a cup, a house, a building, a farmer
	모음으로 시작할 때	an apple, an elephant, an office, an umbrella
정관사 the 특정한 명사와 사용 (복수 명사와 사용 가능)	무엇을 가리키는지 알 때	Turn off the light.
	앞에 나온 명사 반복	Tom has a car. The car is fast.
	유일한 것	The sun rises in the east.
	악기 이름 앞	She plays the violin.
	특정 국가 이름, 산맥, 강, 바다, 유명한 건물, 랜드마크	the United States, the Nile, the Eiffel Tower
관사를 쓰지 않는 경우	식사, 운동, 교통	I have breakfast at 8 a.m. She goes to work by bus.
	장소가 본래의 목적으로 쓰일 때	go to school / go to church

D 다음 빈칸에 a, an, the 중 알맞은 것을 쓰시오. (단, 한 번씩만 쓸 것)

1 He is looking for _____ new job.

2 I want to become _____ engineer.

3 She saw an elephant. _____ elephant was big.

혼공연습

A 다음 괄호 안에서 알맞은 것을 고르시오.

1 I eat (apple / an apple).

2 You drive (car / a car) to work.

3 He reads (book / a book) every day.

4 She finds (joy / a joy) in small things.

5 Plants need (water / a water).

6 We went to (New York / a New York) yesterday.

7 My sister buys (soap / a soap) at that store.

8 A bird sits on (tree / a tree).

B 다음 명사의 복수형을 쓰시오.

1 map → _____	2 pen → _____
3 box → _____	4 flower → _____
5 desk → _____	6 bus → _____
7 dish → _____	8 bench → _____
9 church → _____	10 hero → _____
11 baby → _____	12 city → _____
13 country → _____	14 candy → _____
15 hobby → _____	16 story → _____
17 leaf → _____	18 knife → _____
19 life → _____	20 thief → _____

C 다음 문장의 밑줄 친 부분을 알맞은 복수형으로 바꿔 쓰시오.

1 She washes her <u>foots</u>. → _____

2 The <u>childs</u> play in the park. → _____

3 The <u>mans</u> work together in the factory. → _____

4 He saw two <u>mouses</u> in the kitchen. → _____

5 The <u>gooses</u> fly in the sky. → _____

6 Several <u>fishes</u> were swimming in the aquarium. → _____

D 다음 문장의 밑줄 친 부분을 복수 명사로 바꿔 문장을 다시 쓰시오.

1 We need <u>a chair</u> for the event.

→ _____

2 They watch <u>a movie</u> every weekend.

→ _____

3 My family digs up <u>a potato</u>.

→ _____

4 The wind moves <u>a branch</u>.

→ _____

5 She catches <u>a dragonfly</u> with her net.

→ _____

6 I found <u>a knife</u> on the floor.

→ _____

A 다음 괄호 안에서 알맞은 것을 고르시오.

1 This is (cup / a cup).

2 It is (umbrella / an umbrella).

3 She wears (hat / a hat).

4 He painted (picture / a picture).

5 I like to drink (juice / a juice).

6 I read (story / a story) to my sister.

7 (Honey / A honey) is sweet and delicious.

8 (Milk / A milk) is good for your health.

9 He loves the smell of (coffee / a coffee).

10 They don't know (Suji / a Suji).

11 We hope for (peace / a peace) in the world.

12 Michael showed (kindness / a kindness) to everyone.

13 She adds (sugar / a sugar) to her tea.

14 They bought (bread / a bread) from the bakery.

15 She has (trust / a trust) in her team.

16 (Ice / An ice) melts quickly in the sun.

17 He finds (happiness / a happiness) in his life.

18 I visited (Seoul / a Seoul) last summer.

19 There is (old book / an old book) on the shelf.

20 The beach is covered with (sand / sands).

다음 괄호 안에서 알맞은 것을 고르시오.

1   (Rabbits / A rabbit) are very cute.

2   He bought new (shoe / shoes).

3   I see (star / stars) in the night sky.

4   (Frogs / A frog) is jumping in the pond.

5   He placed three (table / tables) in the corner of the room.

6   Bees love many (flower / flowers) in the garden.

7   He cooks (rice / rices) for dinner.

8   She changed two (tire / tires) on the car.

9   Sam cut the (wood / woods) into pieces.

10   The cake is made from (flour / flours).

11   I gave him (love / loves).

12   She received many (present / presents).

13   She drew a picture on (paper / papers).

14   He writes (letter / letters) to his sister.

15   I exchanged (gold / golds) for money.

16   He selected many (place / places) to visit in the city.

17   They went outside for fresh (air / airs).

18   We removed (pin / pins) from the wall.

19   (Silver / Silvers) is expensive.

20   We think (honesty / honesties) makes our society a better place.

C 다음 괄호 안에서 알맞은 것을 고르시오.

1 I like to play with my (friends / friendes).

2 I didn't take many (classs / classes).

3 They sat on the (benchs / benches) in the park.

4 The teacher taught English to (students / studentes).

5 The (ladys / ladies) are waiting their turns.

6 (Foxs / Foxes) are wild animals.

7 She printed (copys / copies) of the report for the meeting.

8 Grandma always tells us funny (storys / stories).

9 (Leafs / Leaves) fall in autumn.

10 (Typhoons / Typhoones) are very dangerous.

11 (Bananas / Bananaes) are my favorite fruit.

12 Our town has two (librarys / libraries).

13 There are many (tomato / tomatoes) on the vines.

14 I can hear the (birds / birdes) singing.

15 Two (armys / armies) faced each other on the field.

16 Many tourists love the (beachs / beaches) in Jeju Island.

17 Nurses are the real (heros / heroes) of our time.

18 She bought some fresh (potatos / potatoes) from the market.

19 Digital (pianos / pianoes) are popular for beginners.

20 My friends took (photos / photoes) in the museum.

D 다음 대화의 괄호 안에서 알맞은 것을 고르시오.

1   A: Look at those (cloud / clouds) in the sky!

        B: They look like animals.

2   A: What kinds of (jobs / jobes) do people have?

        B: Many people work in factories.

3   A: Did you see the (geese / gooses) flying over the lake?

        B: Yes, they looked so beautiful.

4   A: Where are your (keys / keyes)?

        B: They are on the table.

5   A: Why are there so many (hat / hats) on the sofa?

        B: My friends brought them for the costume party.

6   A: Did he win the (race / races)?

        B: Yes, it was a difficult one for him.

7   A: Why is the (water / waters) so cold today?

        B: The heater might be broken.

8   A: Why do you always write in those (diary / diaries)?

        B: It helps me clear my mind.

9   A: Are the (mice / mouse) eating the bread again?

        B: Yeah, we need to keep our food in a box.

혼공실전 ㄹ

A 다음 우리말에 맞도록 괄호 안의 단어를 이용하여 빈칸에 알맞은 복수 명사를 쓰시오.

1   박쥐들이 동굴 속으로 숨고 있다. (bat)

→ The _____ are hiding inside a cave.

2   아이들은 종이로 비행기들을 만들었다. (plane)

→ The children made _____ out of paper.

3   그 슈퍼히어로에게는 많은 강력한 적들이 있다. (enemy)

→ The superhero has many powerful _____.

4   이 박물관에는 공룡들의 뼈가 전시되어 있다. (bone)

→ This museum has _____ of dinosaurs on display.

5   내 친구는 그의 생일에 새 장난감들을 받았다. (toy)

→ My friend got new _____ for his birthday.

6   그는 붓들로 울타리를 칠했다. (brush)

→ He painted the fence with _____.

7   나의 어머니는 어제 물고기 몇 마리를 잡으셨다. (fish)

→ My mother caught some _____ yesterday.

8   어젯밤 하늘에는 불꽃놀이가 아름다웠다. (firework)

→ The _____ were beautiful in the sky last night.

9   그 여자들은 축제를 준비하고 있다. (woman)

→ The _____ are preparing for the festival.

10   나무에는 초록색 잎들이 많이 있었다. (leaf)

→ There were many green _____ on the tree.

B 다음 빈칸에 a, an, the 중 알맞은 것을 쓰시오.

1 I saw _____ apple on the table. (특정하지 않은 사과)

2 They found _____ boat near the river. (특정하지 않은 배)

3 _____ moon is very bright tonight.

4 He learned how to play _____ guitar.

5 We visited a park near our home. _____ park was very beautiful.

6 I saw a man walking a dog. _____ man looked very tired.

7 He wants to buy _____ sandwich for breakfast. (특정하지 않은 샌드위치)

8 He opened a new restaurant. _____ restaurant is famous for its desserts.

9 There is _____ car parked in front of my house. (특정하지 않은 차)

10 I saw a picture of _____ Great Wall of China in a book.

11 A boy played with a ball. _____ boy looked very happy.

12 She dreams of becoming _____ astronaut one day.

13 We visited _____ Eiffel Tower during our trip to Paris.

14 Jane bought _____ house near the beach. (특정하지 않은 집)

15 I found _____ interesting article online. (특정하지 않은 기사)

16 I am planning to visit _____ museum tomorrow. (특정하지 않은 박물관)

17 She needs _____ hour to complete her work.

18 There is _____ cat sleeping on the couch. (특정하지 않은 고양이)

19 She planted _____ unusual flower in the garden. (특정하지 않은 꽃)

20 I met _____ artist during my vacation. (특정하지 않은 예술가)

C 다음 문장의 밑줄 친 부분을 복수 명사로 바꿔 문장을 다시 쓰시오.

1   He collected a shell from the beach.

→ _____

2   She drew a fish in her notepad.

→ _____

3   A chef prepared a dish for his guests.

→ _____

4   They found a footprint in the sand.

→ _____

5   She caught a mouse in the attic.

→ _____

6   She adopted a puppy from the shelter.

→ _____

7   A hunter saw a deer in the forest.

→ _____

8   He bought a watch from the market.

→ _____

9   We saw an ox in the field.

→ _____

10   A teacher corrected a mistake in the students' homework.

→ _____

11   We visited a church built in the 18th century.

→ _____

12   I could hear an echo in the large cave.

→ _____

13   A fisherman caught a salmon in the river.

→ _____

14   She found a bridge between the two cities.

→ _____

15   A boy saw a witch in his book.

→ _____

D 다음 문장의 밑줄 친 부분을 어법에 맞게 고쳐 문장을 다시 쓰시오.

1 He used <u>a butter</u> to bake the cake.

→ _____

2 I watched a documentary about <u>a Leonardo da Vinci</u>.

→ _____

3 The soup needs <u>salts</u>.

→ _____

4 He spilled <u>inks</u> on his notebook.

→ _____

5 <u>A Colosseum</u> in Rome is an iconic landmark.

→ _____

6 There wasn't much <u>snows</u> on the road this morning.

→ _____

7 <u>Sahara Desert</u> is in North Africa.

→ _____

8 <u>A NASA</u> is planning to send people to Mars.

→ _____

9 He is full of <u>a hope</u> for the future.

→ _____

10 He has a lot of <u>knowledges</u> about science.

→ _____

11 <u>A patience</u> is the key to success.

→ _____

12 She felt deep <u>sadnesses</u> at that time.

→ _____

13 <u>Rains</u> can make flowers grow quickly.

→ _____

14 She wiped the table to remove <u>dusts</u>.

→ _____

15 My sweater is made of soft <u>wools</u>.

→ _____

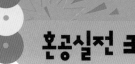

1 다음 중 명사의 복수형이 잘못 짝지어진 것은?

① dog - dogs

② box - boxs

③ baby - babies

④ party - parties

⑤ life – lives

4

A: Look at the _____ on the tree!

B: They are moving so fast.

① monkeyies   ② monkies

③ monkes   ④ monkeys

⑤ monkeyes

[2-4] 다음 중 빈칸에 들어갈 말로 가장 적절한 것을 고르시오.

2

I saw _____ interesting movie last night.

① a   ② an

③ any   ④ many

⑤ 없음

[5-6] 다음 중 빈칸에 들어갈 알맞은 관사를 쓰시오.

5

나는 물 한 잔이 필요하다.

→ I need _____ glass of water.

3

A: I need to clean the _____ in my room.

B: Why? Are they dirty?

① shelf   ② shelfs

③ shelfes   ④ shelf's

⑤ shelves

6

그녀는 그 파티에서 입을 드레스를 샀다.
그 드레스는 파란색이고 아주 아름다웠다.

→ She bought a dress for the party.
_____ dress was blue and very
beautiful.

7

A: I found _____ wallet on the bus.
B: Did you return _____ wallet to its owner?

① a - a
② a - the
③ an - an
④ the - a
⑤ the - an

8

A: She sent me _____ email about the project.
B: I see. _____ email may have important details.

① a - A
② a - The
③ an - An
④ an - The
⑤ the - A

9 다음 문장에서 어법상 틀린 곳을 찾아 바르게 고치시오.

He had a idea about the plan.

_____ → _____

[10-11] 다음 우리말에 맞도록 괄호 안의 단어들을 바르게 배열하시오.

10

그는 빵 한 덩어리를 주문했다.
(ordered / he / bread / a loaf of / .)

→ _____

11

그녀는 수프 한 그릇을 준비했다.
(prepared / a bowl of / she / soup / .)

→ _____

12 다음 대화의 빈칸에 공통으로 들어갈 말로 가장 적절한 것은?

A: Did you read about _____ Statue of Liberty?
B: Yes, _____ Statue of Liberty was a gift from France.

① a   ② an
③ the   ④ some
⑤ any

13 다음 중 밑줄 친 부분이 어법상 **틀린** 것은?

① My father found <u>foxes</u> in a trap.

② How many <u>houses</u> are there?

③ The country is rich in <u>rubber</u>.

④ <u>Chocolate</u> is my favorite flavor.

⑤ <u>A happiness</u> is the key to a healthy life.

[16-17] 다음 괄호 안의 주어진 단어 중 알맞은 것을 골라 문장을 다시 쓰시오.

16

I saw (a / an) silver ring on the counter.

→ _____

17

He plays (a / an / the) drum every evening.

→ _____

[14-15] 다음 문장에서 어법상 **틀린** 곳을 찾아 바르게 고치시오.

14

My friend lost two of his front tooth in an accident.

_____ → _____

15

The women in the photo is my aunt.

_____ → _____

18 다음 글의 밑줄 친 부분 중 어법상 **틀린** 곳은?

My dad likes to drink ①<u>cup</u> of coffee. Also, he always reads ②<u>a book</u> in the morning. Sometimes, he eats ③<u>an</u> egg with toast for breakfast. On weekends, he plays ④<u>the guitar</u> and sings with us. In the evening, he likes to watch ⑤<u>a movie</u> or read a book.

①   ②   ③   ④   ⑤

[19-20] 다음 대화에서 어법상 틀린 곳을 찾아 바르게 고치시오.

19

A: We bought many piece of cake from a shop.

B: Which flavors did you buy?

_____ → _____

20

A: I found batteries in a small box.

B: A batteries are for the clock.

_____ → _____

21 다음 대화의 빈칸에 들어갈 말로 가장 적절한 것은?

A: What are those animals near the river?

B: They are _____.

① duckes and geese

② ducks and geese

③ duckies and goose

④ ducks and gooses

⑤ duckes and gooses

22 다음 대화의 빈칸 ⓐ와 ⓑ에 공통으로 들어갈 말이 바르게 짝지어진 것은?

• A: What do you love most about traveling?

B: I love visiting new ⓐ_____ and meeting different ⓑ_____.

• A: What pictures do you usually take during your travels?

B: I take pictures of many famous ⓐ_____ and kind ⓑ_____.

	ⓐ	ⓑ
①	place	- person
②	person	- place
③	places	- people
④	person	- place
⑤	places	- persones

23 다음 글의 빈칸에 공통으로 들어갈 말로 가장 적절한 것은?

Once upon a time, a farmer lived in a small house. One day, he found an egg under a tree. He took _____ egg home and put it in a basket. The next morning, he saw a golden egg in the basket. The egg shone beautifully. The farmer sold _____ golden egg and became rich.

① a   ② an

③ the   ④ some

⑤ any

7

대명사

인칭대명사의 격

수	인칭	주격 (~은, 는, 이, 가)	소유격 (~의)	목적격 (~을 / 를, ~에게)
단수	1인칭	I	my	me
	2인칭	you	your	you
	3인칭	he	his	him
		she	her	her
		it	its	it
복수	1인칭	we	our	us
	2인칭	you	your	you
	3인칭	they	their	them

A 다음 괄호 안에서 알맞은 것을 고르시오.

1 (I / You) am a teacher.

2 This is (his / him) book.

3 She called (my / me).

4 He doesn't know (she / her).

소유대명사와 재귀대명사

수	인칭	소유대명사 (~의 것)	재귀대명사 ((그들) 자신)
단수	1인칭	mine	myself
	2인칭	yours	yourself
	3인칭	his	himself
		hers	herself
		-	itself
복수	1인칭	ours	ourselves
	2인칭	yours	yourselves
	3인칭	theirs	themselves

B 다음 대화의 괄호 안에서 알맞은 것을 고르시오.

1 A: Is this pen (your / yours)?

   B: No, it isn't.

2 A: Did you draw a picture of (yours / yourself)?

   B: No, I didn't.

지시대명사 this, that / 비인칭 주어 it

지시대명사 this, that

	단수	복수
가까이 있는 사물이나 사람	this	these
멀리 있는 사물이나 사람	that	those

비인칭 주어 it

날씨	It is raining.
시간	It is 3 o'clock.
요일	It is Monday.
계절	It is winter.
거리	It is 10 miles.
날짜	It is November 24th.
명암	It is dark outside.

C 다음 중 옳은 문장에 동그라미 하시오.

1 This is my keys.　　　( )

　　These are my keys.　　( )

2 This is September 9th.　( )

　　It is September 9th.　　( )

one, some, any

one 일반적인 '하나' 라는 의미	앞에서 언급된 명사와 같은 종류를 나타냄 I don't have a phone. I'll buy one soon.
some, any 약간(의), 몇 개(의)	some: 주로 긍정의 평서문과 권유를 나타내는 의문문에 사용 I met some friends in Canada.
	any: 주로 부정문과 의문문에 사용 Do you have any questions? No, I don't have any questions.

D 다음 빈칸에 one, some, any 중 알맞은 것을 쓰시오.

1 That apple is bitter. Try this sweet _____.

2 She bought _____ oranges in the market.

3 Are there _____ restaurant around here?

A 다음 괄호 안에서 알맞은 것을 고르시오.

1 (She / Her) is my best friend.

2 I know (his / him) name.

3 (They / Them) like my idea.

4 We enjoy (our / us) time together.

5 She told (I / me) her story.

6 He forgot (his / him) homework.

7 Joel showed (she / her) photos.

8 She invited (us / our) to her birthday party.

B 다음 우리말에 맞도록 괄호 안에서 알맞은 것을 고르시오.

1 이 자리는 그녀의 것이다.
　 → This seat is (her / hers).

2 이 자전거는 내 것이 아니야. 이것은 너의 자전거니?
　 → This bike is not mine. Is this (your / yours)?

3 그는 그의 공책을 잃어버렸어. 저것은 그의 공책이니?
　 → He lost his notebook. Is that (him / his)?

4 당신은 파티에서 즐거운 시간을 보냈나요?
　 → Did you enjoy (you / yourself) at the party?

5 그들은 식사를 모두 스스로 준비했다.
　 → They prepared the meal all by (their / themselves).

C 다음 문장의 밑줄 친 부분을 알맞은 형태로 바꿔 쓰시오.

1 <u>This</u> are my favorite shoes.   → _____

2 <u>That</u> are the houses we live in.   → _____

3 <u>This</u> is raining outside.   → _____

4 <u>That</u> is time to go to bed.   → _____

5 <u>That</u> was very hot yesterday.   → _____

6 <u>That</u> isn't far from the library to the café. → _____

D 다음 문장의 밑줄 친 부분을 알맞은 형태로 바꿔 문장을 다시 쓰시오.

1 This shirt is small, so I'll buy a bigger <u>that</u>.

   → _____

2 The old car was noisy, but this <u>ones</u> is quiet.

   → _____

3 They have <u>any</u> books for you.

   → _____

4 There are <u>any</u> bananas in the basket.

   → _____

5 I don't want <u>some</u> dessert after dinner.

   → _____

6 Did you have <u>some</u> trouble finding the hotel?

   → _____

A 다음 괄호 안에서 알맞은 것을 고르시오.

1   (He / His) is a firefighter.

2   (She / Her) has a little sister.

3   (It / They) are my parents.

4   (We / Our) are teammates.

5   (She / They) is talented.

6   (I / You) am going to the park.

7   (They / Them) play tennis.

8   She helped (us / our).

9   I saw (she / her) in the classroom.

10   She gave (I / me) a gift.

11   I don't know (they / them).

12   The dog looked at (he / him).

13   She thanked (his / him) for his support.

14   The chef prepared a special meal for (we / us).

15   The kids followed (she / her).

16   This is (I / my) birthday cake.

17   She is looking for (she / her) phone.

18   I met (his / him) parents yesterday.

19   The puppy is eating (it / its) food.

20   They are cleaning (their / theirs) room.

다음 괄호 안에서 알맞은 것을 고르시오.

1   This book is (my / mine).

2   That pencil is (your / yours).

3   This device is (his / him).

4   These shoes are (our / ours).

5   These tickets are (her / hers).

6   That guidebook isn't (their / theirs).

7   I think this camera is (her / hers).

8   The food on the plate is (our / ours).

9   These headphones are not (their / theirs).

10   The map on the table is not (his / him).

11   I fixed my car by (me / myself).

12   He cooked for (his / himself).

13   He ate the whole pizza by (him / himself).

14   She changed the tire by (hers / herself).

15   We planted the trees by (ours / ourselves).

16   They washed (they / themselves) after the long hike.

17   He taught (his / himself) to drive a car.

18   She introduced (she / herself) to her new classmates.

19   He prepared (him / himself) for the big test.

20   I trained (me / myself) to wake up early.

C **다음 괄호 안에서 알맞은 것을 고르시오.**

1   (This / These) is a cup.

2   (That / Those) are my favorite flowers.

3   (This / These) bags are heavy.

4   Look at (that / those) beautiful flowers.

5   We can rest under (this / these) tree.

6   (That / Those) are the pants I tried on.

7   Is (that / those) your mug on the table?

8   Are (that / those) curtains new?

9   (This / These) are the tickets for the 8:30 bus.

10   (That / Those) are my bags near the bench.

11   (It / This) is 8 o'clock now.

12   (It / This) is cold in winter.

13   (It / That) is very dark in the room.

14   (It / That) is March 24th.

15   (It / That) is 3 kilometers from here to the school.

16   (It / That) snows a lot in winter.

17   (It / There) are two bottles on the table.

18   (It / These) is very bright outside.

19   (It / This) will be summer soon.

20   (It / This) isn't 2:30 now.

D 다음 대화의 괄호 안에서 알맞은 것을 고르시오.

1   A: Do you need a bag?
    B: No, I already have (any / one).

2   A: Do you have (any / one) tomatoes?
    B: No, I don't.

3   A: Are there (some / any) trains to Paris tonight?
    B: Yes, but (some / any) of them are fully booked.

4   A: Do you need any help with your homework?
    B: Yes, I need (some / any) help.

5   A: Can I have a balloon for my little sister?
    B: Of course, take (one / them) from here.

6   A: Would you like (some / one) snacks for the trip?
    B: Yes, please. Thank you.

7   A: Do you have (one / any) books about science fiction?
    B: No, we don't.

8   A: Would you like another cup of coffee?
    B: Yes, I'll take (one / them).

9   A: Could you give me (some / one) advice on this matter?
    B: Of course. Let's talk about it.

A 다음 우리말에 맞도록 빈칸에 알맞은 말을 쓰시오.

1 나는 책을 읽고 있다.

→ _____ am reading a book.

2 그녀는 나의 수학 선생님이다.

→ _____ is my math teacher.

3 그의 얼굴이 정말 귀엽다.

→ _____ face is very cute.

4 그녀의 머리카락은 정말 길다.

→ _____ hair is very long.

5 우리 정원에는 많은 꽃들이 있다.

→ _____ garden has many flowers.

6 그는 나를 위해 부서진 의자를 고쳤다.

→ He fixed the broken chair for _____.

7 나는 그들에게 나의 여행에 대해 말했다.

→ I told _____ about my trip.

8 그는 우리에게 선물에 대해 고마워했다.

→ He thanked _____ for the gift.

9 엄마는 그녀에게 그녀의 방을 청소하라고 하셨다.

→ Mom asked _____ to clean her room.

10 그녀는 그에게 공을 패스했다.

→ She passed the ball to _____.

B 다음 우리말에 맞도록 빈칸에 알맞은 말을 쓰시오.

1   그 컵은 내 것이다.

   → The cup is _____.

2   이 텐트는 우리 것이 아니다.

   → This tent isn't _____.

3   이 여권은 당신의 것이다.

   → This passport is _____.

4   이 카드는 그들의 것이 아니다.

   → This card is not _____.

5   이 휴대폰은 그녀의 것이다.

   → This phone is _____.

6   밖에 있는 자전거는 그의 것이다.

   → The bike outside is _____.

7   너는 너 자신을 위한 시간이 필요하다.

   → You need time for _____.

8   그녀는 혼자서 과학 프로젝트를 준비했다.

   → She prepared for the science project by _____.

9   우리는 관객들에게 우리를 소개했다.

   → We introduced _____ to the audience.

10   그들은 집을 스스로 청소했다.

   → They cleaned the house by _____.

C 다음 문장의 밑줄 친 부분을 알맞은 형태로 바꿔 문장을 다시 쓰시오.

1   <u>Me</u> am studying English hard.

    → _____

2   <u>His</u> is practicing basketball.

    → _____

3   He is waiting for <u>we</u> at the bus stop.

    → _____

4   The teacher praised <u>his</u> for his presentation skills.

    → _____

5   He left <u>him</u> jacket on the subway.

    → _____

6   Thank you for sharing <u>you</u> story with me.

    → _____

7   <u>Her</u> often visits her grandparents.

    → _____

8   The song reminded <u>he</u> of his childhood.

    → _____

9   The movie made <u>we</u> laugh so much.

    → _____

10 I went to the movies by <u>me</u>.

    → _____

11 <u>His</u> loves ice cream and chocolate.

    → _____

12 She asked <u>I</u> several questions.

    → _____

13 I think this backpack is <u>him</u>.

    → _____

14 You have to solve this problem by <u>you</u>.

    → _____

15 The gray laptop is <u>her</u>.

    → _____

D 다음 문장의 밑줄 친 부분을 알맞은 형태로 바꿔 문장을 다시 쓰시오.

1 Look at <u>that</u> colorful birds.

→ _____

2 <u>Those</u> is a very creative idea.

→ _____

3 <u>This</u> sunglasses don't match my style.

→ _____

4 <u>That</u> takes three hours to get to the hospital.

→ _____

5 <u>This</u> will be sunny all weekend.

→ _____

6 <u>These</u> muffin is delicious. Try it.

→ _____

7 I need <u>any</u> water after exercise.

→ _____

8 Do you have <u>some</u> questions?

→ _____

9 That burger is mine. You can take the smaller <u>that</u>.

→ _____

10 He doesn't have <u>some</u> money in his wallet.

→ _____

11 <u>That</u> is ten miles from here to the airport.

→ _____

12 He doesn't have <u>some</u> friends in this town.

→ _____

13 The teacher gave us <u>any</u> homework.

→ _____

14 <u>That</u> was foggy this morning.

→ _____

15 This book is boring. Let's read a fun <u>that</u>.

→ _____

[1-3] **다음 중 빈칸에 들어갈 말로 가장 적절한 것을 고르시오.**

1

He taught _____ chess.

① he　　　　② his
③ she　　　　④ they
⑤ us

2

He didn't bring _____ textbook for today's class.

① me　　　　② him
③ hers　　　　④ his
⑤ mine

3

Is this bike _____ or his?

① mine　　　　② her
③ your　　　　④ you
⑤ their

[4-5] **다음 우리말에 맞도록 빈칸에 알맞은 말을 쓰시오.**

4

저 우산은 그녀의 것이 아니다.

→ That umbrella isn't _____.

5

그 마을까지 3킬로미터이다.

→ _____ is three kilometers to the town.

6 **다음 중 밑줄 친 부분이 어법상 틀린 것은?**

① This is <u>her</u> eraser.
② He rides <u>his</u> horse.
③ <u>Our</u> team won the game.
④ She gave <u>me</u> a book.
⑤ He told <u>our</u> a story.

7

다음 대화의 빈칸에 들어갈 말이 바르게 짝지어진 것은?

A: Did you finish _____ homework?
B: Yes, I finished _____ yesterday.

① your - it
② his - him
③ my - its
④ his - my
⑤ your - your

[8-9] **다음 중 빈칸에 들어갈 말로 알맞지 <u>않은</u> 것을 고르시오.**

8

Her advice helped _____ a lot.

① me   ② you
③ his   ④ her
⑤ us

9

This car is _____.

① mine   ② yours
③ his   ④ hers
⑤ their

[10-11] **다음 문장에서 어법상 <u>틀린</u> 곳을 찾아 바르게 고치시오.**

10

Those birds built its nests.

_____ → _____

11

Jane, did you do your homework by you?

_____ → _____

12 다음 글의 밑줄 친 부분 중 어법상 <u>틀린</u> 곳은?

Tom loves ①<u>his</u> mom very much. Tom's mom helps ②<u>him</u> every day. She takes care of ③<u>he</u> with love. Tom is thankful for ④<u>her</u> kindness. He will write ⑤<u>her</u> a thank-you letter.

①   ②   ③   ④   ⑤

13 다음 빈칸에 공통으로 들어갈 말로 적절한 것은?

> • _____ is already dark outside.
> • _____ was Tuesday yesterday.

① It ② That
③ This ④ These
⑤ Those

14 다음 중 어법상 옳은 것은?

① I saw himself at the library.
② He favorite color is blue.
③ I borrowed she books.
④ His house is near the park.
⑤ I want to hear you opinion.

15 다음 괄호 안의 주어진 단어 중 알맞은 것을 골라 문장을 다시 쓰시오.

> The blue car is not (they / their / theirs).

→ _____

[16-18] 다음 우리말에 맞도록 빈칸에 알맞은 말을 보기 에서 골라 쓰시오.

> 보기   one   some   any

16

> 이 수건은 젖었어. 나는 마른 것이 필요해.

→ This towel is wet. I need a dry _____ .

17

> 그녀는 집에 가는 길에 어떤 새도 보지 못했다.

→ She didn't see _____ bird on her way home.

18

> 나는 뒷마당에 나무 몇 그루를 심었다.

→ I planted _____ trees in my backyard.

[19-20] **다음 문장의 밑줄 친 부분을 어법상 바르게 고쳐 문장을 다시 쓰시오.**

19 <u>These</u> orange is so fresh and sweet.

→ _____

20 <u>That</u> are my favorite songs.

→ _____

21 **다음 질문에 대한 대답으로 가장 적절한 것은?**

A: Do you want a white shirt?
B: _____

① No, I want it.

② Yes, I don't like one.

③ No, I want a black one.

④ No, I want a white one.

⑤ Yes, I don't want a shirt.

22 **다음 두 대화의 각 빈칸에 들어갈 알맞은 말을 쓰시오.**

(1) A: What is your brother's name?
   B: _____ name is Joel.
(2) A: Where is my wallet?
   B: _____ is on the desk.

(1) → _____

(2) → _____

23 **다음 글의 빈칸에 들어갈 말이 바르게 짝지어진 것은?**

Sam is one of my best friends. One day, he gave _____ a small notebook as a gift. He said, "Use this to write _____ thoughts and dreams." I write in it every night before bed. Thanks to Sam, I now have a place to write down the stories of my life.

① my – you

② my – your

③ me – you

④ me – your

⑤ myself – your

8

의문문

의문사가 없는 의문문

일반동사의 의문문	Do / Does / Did + 주어 + 동사원형 ~? Does she like apples? → Yes, she does. / No, she doesn't.
be동사의 의문문	Be동사(am, are, is, was, were) + 주어 ~? Is he at home? → Yes, he is. / No, he isn't.
조동사의 의문문	조동사 + 주어 + 동사원형 ~? Can you swim? → Yes, I can. / No, I can't.

A 다음 괄호 안에서 알맞은 것을 고르시오.

1 (Is / Are) you ready for the meeting?

2 (Is / Are) it raining outside?

3 (Do / Does) you like coffee?

4 (Do / Does) he work from home?

5 (Is / Can) you play the drum?

의문사 who, what, when

Who (누구, 누가)	Who is that boy? → He is my brother. (Yes or No 대답 X) Who teaches your English class?
What (무엇, 무슨)	What is on the table? What does it mean?
When (언제)	When is your birthday? When do you go to the gym?

B 다음 대화의 괄호 안에서 알맞은 것을 고르시오.

1 A: (Who / What) is your best friend?

   B: My best friend is Jake.

2 A: (When / What) does the next bus leave?

   B: It leaves in 10 minutes.

Where (어디에, 어디에서)	Where is my phone? Where did you go last weekend?
Why (왜)	Why are they late? Why did she say that?
How (어떤, 어떻게)	How is the weather? How do you cook this dish?
	How + many, much, tall, far, long, often (얼마나 ~한(하게)) How many friends do you have?

C 다음 중 옳은 문장에 동그라미 하시오.

1 Why is the bus stop?　　( )

   Where is the bus stop?　( )

2 How do you bake bread? ( )

   What do you bake bread? ( )

3 Where are your friends?　( )

   When are your friends?　( )

선택의문문	주어진 선택지 중 하나를 고르도록 묻는 의문문
	Do you like apples or oranges? → I like apples. Which do you like better, summer or winter? → I like summer better.
부가의문문	동의를 구하거나 확인할 때 사용하는 의문문
	You like pasta, don't you? → Yes, I do. / No, I don't. He isn't a doctor, is he? → Yes, he is. / No, he isn't.

D 다음 대화의 괄호 안에서 알맞은 것을 고르시오.

1 A: (Which / Where) color do you like better, red or blue?

   B: I like red better.

2 A: He is from Canada, (is / isn't) he?

   B: (Yes / No), he is.

3 A: She likes chocolate, (does / doesn't) she?

   B: (Yes / No), she doesn't.

혼공연습

A 다음 괄호 안에서 알맞은 것을 고르시오.

1 (Is / Are) you in the library?

2 (Is / Are) she a nurse?

3 (Do / Does) they know each other?

4 (Do / Does) he like cheese?

5 (Do / Does) Joel change his hairstyle often?

6 (Is / Can) she solve this math problem?

7 (Are / Will) you come to the party tonight?

8 (Am / Should) I prepare dinner now?

B 다음 대화의 빈칸에 알맞은 의문사를 쓰시오.

1 A: _____ can I get to the train station?

   B: Go straight and turn left.

2 A: _____ does your brother study?

   B: He studies at home.

3 A: _____ does the movie start?

   B: It starts in 15 minutes.

4 A: _____ wrote this book?

   B: J. K. Rowling wrote it.

5 A: _____ are you happy?

   B: I am happy because the weather is nice.

C 다음 밑줄 친 부분을 우리말에 맞도록 알맞은 의문사로 고쳐 쓰시오.

1 <u>What</u> are you sad? (너는 왜 슬퍼하니?)　　　　　→ ＿＿＿＿＿＿

2 <u>When</u> is your hat? (너의 모자는 어디 있니?)　　　　→ ＿＿＿＿＿＿

3 <u>Who</u> is your brother's name? (너의 형 이름이 뭐니?)　→ ＿＿＿＿＿＿

4 <u>What</u> will you be back? (너는 언제 돌아올 거니?)　　→ ＿＿＿＿＿＿

5 <u>Why</u> long does it take? (시간이 얼마나 걸리니?)　　→ ＿＿＿＿＿＿

6 <u>Where</u> has my notebook? (누가 내 공책을 가지고 있니?)　→ ＿＿＿＿＿＿

D 다음 대화의 빈칸에 들어갈 알맞은 말을 쓰시오.

1 A: You are studying for the test, aren't you?

　B: Yes, ＿＿＿＿＿＿ ＿＿＿＿＿＿.

2 A: She is a science teacher, isn't she?

　B: No, ＿＿＿＿＿＿ ＿＿＿＿＿＿.

3 A: It wasn't too expensive, was it?

　B: No, ＿＿＿＿＿＿ ＿＿＿＿＿＿.

4 A: You live near here, don't you?

　B: No, ＿＿＿＿＿＿ ＿＿＿＿＿＿.

5 A: He doesn't know about this, does he?

　B: Yes, ＿＿＿＿＿＿ ＿＿＿＿＿＿.

6 A: They changed the schedule, didn't they?

　B: No, ＿＿＿＿＿＿ ＿＿＿＿＿＿.

A 다음 괄호 안에서 알맞은 것을 고르시오.

1 (Is / are) Jake a good student?

2 (Do / Does) you understand the lessons?

3 (Is / Are) you happy with the result?

4 (Can / Do) he drive a car?

5 (Is / Are) she a good singer?

6 (Am / Can) I borrow your pen?

7 (Do / Does) he have a textbook for this class?

8 (Does / Should) we climb the mountain?

9 (Was / Were) he surprised at the birthday party?

10 (Did / Is) she pass the math test?

11 (Was / Were) he angry this morning?

12 (Do / Does) we have tickets for the concert?

13 (Do / Did) you call me yesterday?

14 (Do / Does) Mike remember my birthday?

15 (Is / Will) he follow the rules?

16 (Does / Did) they win the game?

17 (Did / Were) they invite us to the event?

18 (Do / Does) Sam speak other languages?

19 (Was / Were) I a good friend to you?

20 (Can / Do) Michael join us for dinner tonight?

B 다음 괄호 안에서 알맞은 것을 고르시오.

1   (Who / What) can I do for you?

2   (Who / Where) does he work?

3   (Why / What) did she cry?

4   (What / When) did it happen?

5   (Why / How) was the movie?

6   (Who / Why) is she upset today?

7   (Who / How) can I use this app?

8   (How / What) are they talking about?

9   (Who / How) wants to join the team?

10   (Who / Why) is this important?

11   (Who / How) told you that story?

12   (Who / When) is responsible for this accident?

13   (Who / Why) do humans dream?

14   (Who / When) should we leave for the airport?

15   (What / Which) are you doing now?

16   (Who / What) can we learn from this experience?

17   (What / Where) can I buy fresh vegetables?

18   (When / Where) is the best place to see the stars?

19   (What / Why) do some birds fly south in winter?

20   (Who / How) do magicians perform their tricks?

C 다음 괄호 안에서 알맞은 것을 고르시오.

1 How (many / much) apples are in the basket?

2 How (long / thick) is your summer vacation?

3 How (often / old) do you drink coffee?

4 How (many / much) is this shirt?

5 How (many / long) does it take to get to the hospital?

6 How (old / long) are your grandparents?

7 How (often / much) do you eat out?

8 How (far / often) is your house from school?

9 How (tall / often) is the Eiffel Tower?

10 How (many / much) people live in your city?

11 How (far / often) is the Sun from the Earth?

12 How (often / far) do you watch TV?

13 How (far / tall) can a bird fly without resting?

14 How (tall / often) are giraffes on average?

15 How (often / many) do you meet your friends?

16 How (far / many) can you throw a ball?

17 How (many / much) did you pay for your computer?

18 How (many / long) can you hold your breath?

19 How (many / much) days do you work in a week?

20 How (long / often) does it take to finish the book?

D 다음 대화의 괄호 안에서 알맞은 것을 고르시오.

1   A: (Which / Why) do you prefer, dogs or cats?

    B: I prefer cats to dogs.

2   A: Do you go to school by bus (or / and) by bicycle?

    B: I go to school by bus.

3   A: (Which / How) sport do you enjoy more, soccer or baseball?

    B: I enjoy baseball more.

4   A: It is the correct answer, (is / isn't) it?

    B: Yes, it (is / isn't).

5   A: The door isn't locked, (is / isn't) it?

    B: No, it (is / isn't).

6   A: The kids were playing in the backyard, (were / weren't) they?

    B: Yes, they (were / weren't).

7   A: It snows heavily, (does / doesn't) it?

    B: No, it (does / doesn't).

8   A: We don't need any more milk, (do / don't) we?

    B: Yes, we (do / don't).

9   A: He booked the tickets for the trip, (did / didn't) he?

    B: Yes, he (did / didn't).

혼공실전 2

A 다음 우리말에 맞도록 빈칸에 알맞은 말을 쓰시오.

1 당신은 음악가인가요?

→ _____ you a musician?

2 그녀가 당신의 어머니인가요?

→ _____ she your mother?

3 이것은 좋은 생각인가요?

→ _____ this a good idea?

4 어제 시험이 어려웠나요?

→ _____ the test hard yesterday?

5 당신은 자전거를 탈 수 있나요?

→ _____ you ride a bike?

6 그는 매일 밤에 공부하나요?

→ _____ he study every night?

7 그들이 음악을 듣고 있나요?

→ _____ they listening to music?

8 그들은 매주 일요일에 농구를 하나요?

→ _____ they play basketball on Sundays?

9 어젯밤 음식이 마음에 들었나요?

→ _____ you like the food last night?

10 제가 진실을 말해야 할까요?

→ _____ I tell the truth?

B 다음 우리말에 맞도록 빈칸에 알맞은 말을 쓰시오.

1 그것은 무슨 뜻인가요?

→ ＿＿＿＿＿＿＿＿ does it mean?

2 당신의 롤모델은 누구인가요?

→ ＿＿＿＿＿＿＿＿ is your role model?

3 당신은 언제 잠자리에 드나요?

→ ＿＿＿＿＿＿＿＿ do you go to bed?

4 당신은 휴가를 어디에서 보내나요?

→ ＿＿＿＿＿＿＿＿ do you spend your holidays?

5 이 일이 끝난 후에는 무슨 일이 일어날까요?

→ ＿＿＿＿＿＿＿＿ will happen after this?

6 당신은 어떻게 체중을 감량하나요?

→ ＿＿＿＿＿＿＿＿ do you lose weight?

7 우리는 왜 지금 갈 수 없나요?

→ ＿＿＿＿＿＿＿＿ can't we go now?

8 이 편지는 누가 썼나요?

→ ＿＿＿＿＿＿＿＿ wrote this letter?

9 당신은 2주 전에 어디로 여행 갔나요?

→ ＿＿＿＿＿＿＿＿ did you travel two weeks ago?

10 당신이 가장 좋아하는 영화는 무엇인가요?

→ ＿＿＿＿＿＿＿＿ is your favorite movie?

C 다음 괄호 안의 단어들을 바르게 배열하여 의문문을 만드시오.

1 (is / who / he / ?)

→ _____

2 (are / what / you / doing / ?)

→ _____

3 (is / she / why / happy / ?)

→ _____

4 (is / my / laptop / where / ?)

→ _____

5 (why / the sky / blue / is / ?)

→ _____

6 (your parents / how / are / ?)

→ _____

7 (want / what / do / you / to do / ?)

→ _____

8 (why / she / does / laugh / ?)

→ _____

9 (do / know / you / him / ?)

→ _____

10 (how / I / can / you / help / ?)

→ _____

11 (knows / who / the answer / ?)

→ _____

12 (is / old / how / this tree / ?)

→ _____

13 (when / you / will / graduate / ?)

→ _____

14 (how / water / much / do / drink / you / ?)

→ _____

15 (long / how / is / the flight / ?)

→ _____

D 다음 빈칸에 알맞은 말을 써서 부가의문문을 완성하시오.

1   A: You love this song, _____?

    B: Yes, _____.

       No, _____.

2   A: She is your sister, _____?

    B: Yes, _____.

       No, _____.

3   A: The movie is interesting, _____?

    B: Yes, _____.

       No, _____.

4   A: The weather isn't cold, _____?

    B: Yes, _____.

       No, _____.

5   A: This dress doesn't fit you well, _____?

    B: Yes, _____.

       No, _____.

6   A: The event starts early, _____?

    B: Yes, _____.

       No, _____.

7   A: He apologized for the mistake, _____?

    B: Yes, _____.

       No, _____.

8   A: She didn't take your advice, _____?

    B: Yes, _____.

       No, _____.

혼공실전 3

1 다음 우리말에 맞도록 빈칸에 들어갈 말로 적절한 것은?

> • 당신은 어제 무엇을 했나요?
> → _____ did you do yesterday?

① What   ② Who

③ Why   ④ Which

⑤ Where

2 다음 우리말을 바르게 영작한 것은?

> 오늘은 무슨 요일인가요?

① What is your day?

② Where do you live?

③ Who is your teacher?

④ What day is it today?

⑤ Why is it so hot outside?

3 다음 대화의 빈칸에 들어갈 말로 가장 적절한 것은?

> A: _____ are you late?
> B: It is because I missed the bus.

① Who   ② Why

③ When   ④ Where

⑤ How

4 다음 빈칸에 공통으로 들어갈 말로 가장 적절한 것은?

> • _____ long does it take?
> • _____ much does it cost?

① Who   ② How

③ Why   ④ What

⑤ Where

[5-6] 다음 중 밑줄 친 부분이 어법상 <u>틀린</u> 것을 고르시오.

5

① <u>Are</u> you nervous?

② <u>Is</u> he listening to music?

③ <u>Was</u> it noisy last weekend?

④ <u>Are</u> they playing outside?

⑤ <u>Were</u> she a teacher before?

6

① <u>Do</u> I look good?

② <u>Does</u> it work well?

③ <u>Do</u> Mike like animals?

④ <u>Did</u> he call you yesterday?

⑤ <u>Does</u> your mother work outside?

보기

Who   When   Where   What   How   Why

7

A: _____ did you arrive?
B: I got here about an hour ago.

→ _____

8

A: _____ did you have lunch?
B: I ate at the new restaurant.

→ _____

9

A: _____ far is your hometown from here?
B: It's about 300 kilometers away.

→ _____

10 다음 중 밑줄 친 부분의 쓰임이 어색한 것은?

① <u>Who</u> opened the door?

② <u>What</u> is your favorite color?

③ <u>Where</u> should we meet?

④ <u>Why</u> are you working so hard?

⑤ <u>What</u> do the stores open?

11 다음 우리말에 맞도록 빈칸에 알맞은 말을 쓰시오.

입장료는 얼마인가요?

→ _____ much is the entrance fee?

12 다음 대화의 빈칸에 들어갈 말이 바르게 짝지어진 것은?

A: You look upset. _____ are you
   angry?
B: I had a fight with my friends.
A: _____ happened?
B: They said mean things to me.
A: Did you talk to them about it?
B: No, but I will talk to them
   tomorrow.

① What   - When

② What   - Why

③ When   - What

④ Why   - What

⑤ Why   - Who

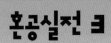

13 다음 문장에서 어법상 <u>틀린</u> 곳을 찾아 바르게 고치시오.

> Which seat do you want, the window and the aisle?

_____ → _____

16 다음 중 짝지어진 대화가 <u>어색한</u> 것은?

① A: What are you doing now?
   B: I'm reading a book.

② A: Why are you so tired?
   B: I didn't sleep well.

③ A: When should I call you?
   B: Call me at 8 o'clock.

④ A: Where is your school?
   B: It's next to the library.

⑤ A: What was your day?
   B: It was a bit stressful.

[14-15] 다음 우리말에 맞도록 괄호 안의 단어들을 바르게 배열하시오.

14

> 당신은 나를 얼마나 사랑하나요?
> (much / how / do / love / you / me / ?)

→ _____

17 다음 대화의 밑줄 친 부분을 어법상 바르게 고치시오.

17

> A: Your sister is a doctor, <u>is</u> she?
> B: No, she isn't.

→ _____

15

> 공항은 여기에서 얼마나 떨어져 있나요?
> (far / how / the airport / is / from / here / ?)

→ _____

18

> A: They enjoyed the trip, <u>do</u> they?
> B: Yes, they did.

→ _____

[19-20] 다음 질문에 대한 대답으로 가장 적절한 것을 고르시오.

19

A: The train is late, isn't it?
B: _____

① Yes, it isn't.
② Yes, it does.
③ No, it is.
④ No, it isn't.
⑤ No, it doesn't.

20

A: He doesn't eat meat, does he?
B: _____

① Yes, he does.
② Yes, he doesn't.
③ No, he is.
④ No, he isn't
⑤ No, he don't.

21 다음 대화의 빈칸에 공통으로 들어갈 알맞은 말을 쓰시오.

A: She doesn't like spicy food, _____ she?
B: Yes, she _____.

→ _____

22 다음 중 밑줄 친 부분의 쓰임이 옳은 것끼리 바르게 짝지어진 것은?

a. <u>When</u> is your birthday?
b. <u>How many</u> will you stay?
c. <u>What</u> do you want to eat?
d. <u>Why</u> do you cry?

① a, b
② a, c
③ b, c
④ b, d
⑤ c, d

23 다음 글의 빈칸 ⓐ~ⓒ에 들어갈 말이 바르게 짝지어진 것은?

My mom always loves me. One day, I asked her, "ⓐ_____ do you always care for me?" She smiled and said, "It is because you're my child." Then I asked, "ⓑ_____ do you rest?" She laughed and said, "I rest constantly." Finally, I asked, "ⓒ_____ does all your love come from?" She held my hand and said, "It comes from my heart." Her words made my day.

	ⓐ	ⓑ	ⓒ
①	What	When	Where
②	What	Why	Where
③	Why	When	Where
④	Why	How	Why
⑤	Why	When	How

혼공
중학 영문법
마스터

Level · 1

_____

정답

_____

혼공개념 pp. 8-9

Ⓐ **1** am **2** are **3** is **4** is **5** are

Ⓑ **1** Am, aren't
2 Is, is

Ⓒ **1** He is not a doctor. (O)
2 It is not cold today. (O)
3 She is not hungry. (O)

Ⓓ **1** Was, was
2 Were, wasn't

혼공연습 pp. 10-11

Ⓐ **1** am **2** are **3** are **4** is **5** is **6** are
7 is **8** are

Ⓑ **1** I'm **2** You're **3** She's **4** It's **5** They're
6 We're **7** isn't **8** isn't

Ⓒ **1** were **2** was **3** were **4** was **5** were
6 was

Ⓓ **1** I am not 15 years old.
2 She is not a teacher.
3 You are not honest.
4 Is he very smart?
5 Are they your best friends?
6 Is the butterfly colorful?

혼공실전 1 pp. 12-15

Ⓐ **1** am **2** are **3** is **4** is **5** is **6** is **7** are
8 is **9** is **10** are **11** is **12** are **13** are
14 are **15** are **16** are **17** is **18** is
19 are **20** are

Ⓑ **1** was **2** was **3** are **4** was **5** was

6 weren't **7** was **8** was **9** is **10** was
11 was **12** is **13** was **14** was **15** was
16 was **17** were **18** were **19** was
20 wasn't

Ⓒ **1** am not **2** aren't **3** isn't **4** aren't
5 isn't **6** isn't **7** aren't **8** isn't **9** isn't
10 I'm not **11** aren't **12** isn't **13** isn't
14 isn't **15** aren't **16** wasn't **17** wasn't
18 weren't **19** weren't **20** weren't

Ⓓ **1** Are, am not
2 Is, is
3 Are, am
4 Is, isn't
5 Are, are
6 Is, is
7 Is, isn't
8 Are, aren't
9 Is, is

혼공실전 2 pp. 16-19

Ⓐ **1** am **2** are **3** are **4** is **5** is **6** is **7** is
8 is **9** were **10** was **11** was **12** were

Ⓑ **1** It's **2** You're **3** We're **4** They're
5 She's **6** isn't **7** aren't **8** aren't **9** isn't
10 wasn't **11** weren't **12** wasn't

Ⓒ **1** You are not[aren't] healthy.
2 I am not angry today.
3 She is not[isn't] a math teacher.
4 We are not[aren't] students.
5 The sky is not[isn't] blue.
6 They are not[aren't] neighbors.
7 The book is not[isn't] interesting.
8 The workers are not[aren't] in a new house.
9 They are not[aren't] members of the science club.
10 The food was not[wasn't] good.
11 The lights were not[weren't] out.
12 The truck was not[wasn't] in the parking lot.

13 I was not[wasn't] curious about the new project.

14 He was not[wasn't] with his friends at the mall.

15 She was not[wasn't] excited about her new job.

D 1 Is the room too small?

2 Are the carts full?

3 Is the line long?

4 Are the books on the shelf?

5 Was she not at school yesterday?

6 Is she always helpful to everyone?

7 Were the students ready for the trip?

8 Are you important to your family?

9 Is she very happy with her job?

10 Was the teacher very friendly?

11 Were the bugs active after rain?

12 Was it a beautiful day for a picnic?

13 Was I in the bookstore for hours?

14 Were the chairs comfortable?

15 Was she thirsty from walking under the hot sun?

옛날 옛적에, 한 왕이 있었다. 그는 슬퍼서, 많은 것을 시도했다. 하지만 아무것도 도움이 되지 않았다. 어느 날, 한 친절한 사람이 그에게 말했다. "행복은 다른 사람을 돕는 데서 옵니다." 그래서, 왕은 진심으로 자신의 백성을 돕기 시작했다. 그는 행복해졌다. 사실, 행복은 항상 그의 마음속에 있었다.

혼공실전 ∃ pp. 20-23

1 ⑤ 2 ⑤ 3 ②

4 The children are in the playground.

5 isn't 6 ② 7 ④ 8 ⑤ 9 is → was

10 ① 11 The weather was warm yesterday.

12 ⑤

나는 중학생이다. 우리 선생님은 매우 친절하시고, 많은 것을 도와주신다. 나는 영어를 잘한다. 하루 중 가장 좋아하는 시간은 영어 수업 시간이다. 내 친구들과 나는 수업시간이 아주 행복하다.

13 am 14 isn't 15 Is

16 ④ 17 is → are 18 was → is

19 Is he in the office?

20 Is John interested in the game?

21 ② 22 ④ 23 ④

CHAPTER 2
문장의 기초 2 (일반동사 편)

A 1 We <u>play</u> soccer.
   2 I <u>run</u> every morning.
   3 He <u>reads</u> a book.
   4 She <u>eats</u> breakfast.

B 1 teaches   2 comes   3 tries   4 finishes
   5 cries

C 1 I do not go to school. (O)
   2 We don't like cucumbers. (O)
   3 She doesn't like it. (O)

D 1 Do, do
   2 Does, doesn't

A 1 runs   2 sleep   3 dances   4 help
   5 grows   6 paint   7 plays   8 rains

B 1 goes   2 does   3 studies   4 flies
   5 goes   6 tries   7 mixes   8 watches

C 1 don't   2 doesn't   3 doesn't   4 don't
   5 doesn't

D 1 He does not[doesn't] drive a blue car.
   2 I do not[don't] sing a song at the party.
   3 Does my dog sit on the bench?
   4 Does she write a letter?
   5 Does he help his father in the garden?

A 1 plays   2 goes   3 runs   4 studies
   5 watches   6 flies   7 reads   8 writes
   9 swims   10 sings   11 jumps   12 catches

   13 fixes   14 teaches   15 wishes
   16 helps   17 dances   18 cries   19 carries
   20 buys   21 makes   22 eats   23 laughs
   24 enjoys   25 gives   26 has   27 does
   28 says   29 needs   30 opens

B 1 watch   2 sets   3 fixes   4 flies   5 paints
   6 dance   7 buy   8 sounds   9 shows
   10 catch   11 studies   12 cooks   13 brush
   14 like   15 wags   16 buys   17 explains
   18 stops   19 drink   20 visit

C 1 doesn't sing   2 don't run
   3 does not play   4 don't chase
   5 doesn't cook   6 doesn't bark
   7 do not watch   8 doesn't fly
   9 don't study   10 does not teach
   11 don't fix   12 do not kick
   13 doesn't drive   14 does not smile
   15 doesn't go   16 does not set
   17 doesn't write   18 does not tell
   19 don't read   20 doesn't love

D 1 Do, do
   2 Does, does
   3 Does, doesn't
   4 Does, does
   5 Does, does
   6 Do, don't
   7 Does, doesn't
   8 Does, does
   9 Does, doesn't

A 1 walk   2 run   3 helps   4 play   5 rains
   6 likes   7 study   8 has   9 barks
   10 works   11 reads   12 writes

B 1 opens   2 watches   3 studies   4 wishes
   5 closes   6 carries   7 hides   8 laughs
   9 tries   10 flies   11 begins   12 goes

C 1 I do not[don't] eat breakfast every morning.

2 She does not[doesn't] drink milk every morning.

3 I do not[don't] watch TV before bed.

4 He does not[doesn't] run fast in the race.

5 You do not[don't] play the guitar very well.

6 He does not[doesn't] read the newspaper daily.

7 You do not[don't] call your friend.

8 He does not[doesn't] check his car every two months.

9 She does not[doesn't] teach English at school.

10 It does not[doesn't] fly over the city.

11 We do not[don't] read books at the library.

12 It does not[doesn't] snow a lot in the winter.

13 We do not[don't] go to the theater on weekends.

14 They do not[don't] study together after school.

15 You do not[don't] write a diary every night.

D 1 Do you drink coffee every morning?

2 Does he wear a hat on sunny days?

3 Do you wait for the bus?

4 Does she exercise at the gym?

5 Do they play soccer on the field?

6 Does it bark loudly at me?

7 Do you walk to school every day?

8 Do they drive to work together?

9 Does she close the door carefully?

10 Do the students learn new things every day?

11 Does he sleep early on weekdays?

12 Does the lion live in the jungle?

13 Does the wind blow softly?

14 Does she buy clothes at the store?

15 Do they swim in the lake?

혼공실전 ㅋ pp. 38-41

1 ④ 2 ② 3 ③ 4 ② 5 doesn't

6 Does 7 ③ 8 ② 9 shine → shines

10 He does not[doesn't] visit my grandmother on Mondays.

11 Do 12 ① 13 don't

14 Do 15 doesn't

16 Do you enjoy spicy food?

17 He doesn't cook dinner for me.

18 Do they go to the library on Sundays?

19 does → doesn't 20 don't → do

21 ⑤ 22 ③ 23 ④

Emily는 빵 굽는 것을 좋아한다. 그녀는 매일 밀가루, 설탕, 그리고 달걀을 섞는다. 그녀의 남동생 Tom은 자신의 방에서 공부한다. 그는 월요일에 시험이 있다. 빵을 다 구우면, Emily는 그에게 쿠키를 나누어 준다.

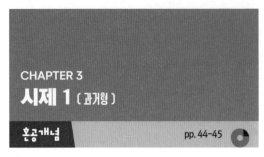

CHAPTER 3
시제 1 (과거형)

혼공개념　　　　　　　　　　pp. 44-45

Ⓐ 1 stopped 2 cried 3 watched 4 liked

Ⓑ 1 He did not like the toy. (O)
  2 We did not play soccer yesterday. (O)
  3 They didn't sing together last week. (O)

Ⓒ 1 Did, did
  2 Did, didn't

혼공연습　　　　　　　　　　pp. 46-47

Ⓐ 1 played 2 drank 3 eat 4 ate
  5 watched 6 went 7 bought 8 worked

Ⓑ 1 worked 2 played 3 talked 4 washed
  5 started 6 loved 7 moved 8 lived
  9 closed 10 hoped 11 cried 12 tried
  13 married 14 carried 15 studied
  16 worried 17 stopped 18 planned
  19 dropped 20 grabbed

Ⓒ 1 liked 2 studied 3 visited 4 cooked
  5 took 6 knew

Ⓓ 1 We did not[didn't] listen to music in the car.
  2 Did she learn new words last night?
  3 They did not[didn't] clean the house last weekend.
  4 I did not[didn't] open the window today.
  5 Did you jump rope yesterday?
  6 Did we find the wrong answer?

혼공실전 1　　　　　　　　　　pp. 48-51

Ⓐ 1 played 2 watched 3 entered
  4 climbed 5 walked 6 shared 7 listened
  8 greeted 9 laughed 10 shouted

11 asked 12 started 13 finished
14 fixed 15 visited 16 traveled 17 met
18 worked 19 hiked 20 enjoyed

Ⓑ 1 went 2 broke 3 drove 4 ate 5 saw
  6 took 7 found 8 ran 9 gave 10 sang
  11 wrote 12 brought 13 bought
  14 knew 15 began 16 drank 17 flew
  18 read 19 kept 20 heard

Ⓒ 1 didn't sing 2 didn't start
  3 didn't change 4 did not join
  5 didn't move 6 didn't swim
  7 did not plan 8 didn't lose 9 didn't eat
  10 didn't write

Ⓓ 1 Did you see a rainbow last spring? (O)
  2 Did they take the bus last night? (O)
  3 Did you read the news this morning? (O)
  4 Did she meet him a long time ago? (O)
  5 Did he leave home early this morning? (O)
  6 Did your father build this treehouse? (O)

Ⓔ 1 Did, did
  2 Did, didn't
  3 watch, did
  4 Did, didn't
  5 travel, did
  6 Did, didn't
  7 Did, did
  8 Did, didn't
  9 Did, did
  10 Did, did

혼공실전 2　　　　　　　　　　pp. 52-55

Ⓐ 1 watched 2 played 3 hiked 4 walked
  5 read 6 drove 7 broke 8 ate 9 wrote
  10 brought 11 taught 12 drank

Ⓑ 1 opened 2 saw[watched] 3 didn't
  4 didn't 5 didn't 6 didn't 7 Did 8 Did
  9 Did 10 Did 11 Did 12 didn't

Ⓒ 1 We did not[didn't] talk about the plan.

2 He did not[didn't] study English last semester.

3 They did not[didn't] wash their car.

4 We did not[didn't] start a new hobby.

5 She did not[didn't] play the piano.

6 They did not[didn't] open a restaurant.

7 I did not[didn't] go to the park yesterday.

8 He did not[didn't] see a rainbow this morning.

9 We did not[didn't] travel to the mountains last winter.

10 I did not[didn't] write a short story last Sunday.

11 We did not[didn't] take photos the day before yesterday.

12 She did not[didn't] eat ice cream last night.

13 They did not[didn't] laugh at the joke.

14 I did not[didn't] buy a new book.

15 They did not[didn't] give me a present last Christmas.

D 1 Did she bake a cake last weekend?

2 Did you listen to music last night?

3 Did she change her job?

4 Did your sister drink lemonade?

5 Did he break his phone?

6 Did he start his guitar lessons?

7 Did she write an essay yesterday?

8 Did they swim in the pool?

9 Did Minsu meet new friends last week?

10 Did you hear a legend?

11 Did she read an article last weekend?

12 Did he run in the race?

13 Did Thomas go to the store yesterday?

14 Did they keep the secret?

15 Did she leave her bag at school?

혼공실전 3 pp. 56–59

1 ④ 2 ⑤ 3 ④ 4 ③
5 ② 6 ② 7 ③ 8 ④
9 The cat grabbed the mouse yesterday.
10 walked → walk 11 read
12 drinks 13 took

14 I saw the sunrise last weekend.

15 We ran in the park this morning.

16 does → did 17 bought → buy

18 Did his friends enjoy the movie?

19 Did they take the bus to school?

20 ④ 21 ③ 22 ④

어제, Emily는 집 열쇠를 잃어버렸다. 그녀는 모든 곳을 찾아보았다. 먼저, 가방을 뒤졌지만, 거기에 없었다. 그런 다음, 부엌을 확인하고, 거실로 갔다. 그녀는 그녀의 남동생에게 물어봤지만, 그도 그것을 보지 못했다.

23 went → go

A: 새로 생긴 가게 봤어?
B: 응, 봤어.
A: 안에 들어가 봤어?
B: 아니, 안 들어가 봤어.
A: 아, 정말? 나 거기서 재킷을 하나 샀어.
B: 가게가 컸어?
A: 응, 컸어.

CHAPTER 4
시제 2 (미래형과 진행형)

혼공개념 pp. 62–63

Ⓐ **1** rain **2** rain **3** going

Ⓑ **1** watching **2** coming **3** sitting **4** dying
5 playing

Ⓒ **1** He is singing now. (O)
2 They were watching TV. (O)

Ⓓ **1** Are, am
2 Were, wasn't

혼공연습 pp. 64–65

Ⓐ **1** call **2** arrive **3** bake **4** open **5** going
6 start **7** Are **8** take

Ⓑ **1** is walking, was walking
2 is talking, was talking
3 is finishing, was finishing
4 is circling, was circling
5 is eating, was eating
6 is hunting, was hunting
7 is running, was running
8 is playing, was playing
9 is sitting, was sitting
10 is reading, was reading

Ⓒ **1** I am reading a book.
2 She is cooking dinner.
3 They are playing soccer.
4 I was running in the morning.
5 She was singing a beautiful song.
6 We were waiting for the bus.

Ⓓ **1** We are not[aren't] watching a movie.
2 The baby is not[isn't] crying loudly.
3 Was my father fixing his bike?

4 Was your sister reading a book?
5 She wasn't cooking dinner.
6 He isn't studying for his exam.

혼공실전 1 pp. 66–69

Ⓐ **1** rain **2** buy **3** invite **4** watch **5** call
6 clean **7** bring **8** going **9** move
10 is **11** bake **12** buy **13** are **14** run
15 read **16** Is **17** Will **18** come **19** help
20 going

Ⓑ **1** walking **2** coming **3** swimming
4 sitting **5** stopping **6** running **7** lying
8 talking **9** jumping **10** playing
11 making **12** writing **13** taking
14 cutting **15** trying **16** applying
17 enjoying **18** practicing **19** buying
20 seeing

Ⓒ **1** are **2** was **3** am **4** was **5** was **6** are
7 are **8** is **9** was **10** was **11** was
12 were **13** was **14** was **15** is **16** was
17 is **18** were **19** was **20** were

Ⓓ **1** Is, is
2 Are, aren't
3 Was, was
4 Were, weren't
5 Were, was
6 Is, is
7 Are, am not
8 Was, wasn't
9 Is, isn't

혼공실전 2 pp. 70–73

Ⓐ **1** will **2** are, going **3** Is, going **4** is, going
5 will **6** is, going **7** Will **8** Are, going
9 Is, going **10** will **11** are, going
12 Is, going

Ⓑ **1** playing **2** kicking **3** drawing
4 sleeping **5** swimming **6** dancing

7 writing **8** learning **9** waiting

10 making **11** lying **12** enjoying

C 1 I am[I'm] having a good time.

2 We are[We're] enjoying good weather.

3 He is[He's] giving her a gift.

4 She is[She's] smiling for the photo.

5 They are[They're] using the computer.

6 They are[They're] staying at a hotel.

7 We were playing at the park.

8 She was painting the walls.

9 I was brushing my teeth.

10 They were planting flowers in the garden.

11 She was washing her hands.

12 We are not[aren't] carrying heavy bags.

13 She is not[isn't] studying in the library.

14 They were not[weren't] shopping at the mall.

15 He was not[wasn't] talking on the phone.

D 1 Will you finish the report by Monday?

2 Will they have lunch together next Friday?

3 Will you study harder for the test?

4 Is she going to study in Canada next year?

5 Are we going to have barbecue tomorrow?

6 Is she sleeping on the sofa?

7 Is he working on a project?

8 Is Youngjoo running on the track?

9 Are they laughing at a clown?

10 Are the dogs sitting by the lake?

11 Was he driving to work?

12 Was she knitting a scarf?

13 Were you making a dress?

14 Were they dancing at the party?

15 Was he reading the newspaper?

혼공실전 3　　　　pp. 74-77

1 ⑤　**2** ③　**3** ③　**4** ④　**5** ②　**6** ④

7 ②　**8** ②, ④　**9** are, going, to

10 were → are　**11** ⑤　**12** ②　**13** is, playing

14 is, sleeping　**15** are, talking

16 A: Is, eating　B: is

17 A: Is　B: isn't, cooking

18 A: Are　B: am, not, solving

19 We are going to start a new project.

20 She was jogging in the park.

21 Was → Were　**22** ④　**23** play → playing

　밖에 비가 내리고 있었다. Jane은 창가에서 책을 읽고 있었다. 그녀의 남동생은 거실에서 비디오 게임을 하고 있었다. 갑자기, 정전이 되었다. 그들은 어둠 속에서 손전등을 찾았다. 그때, 전기가 다시 들어왔다. 그래서 Jane과 그녀의 남동생은 웃었다.

CHAPTER 5
조동사

혼공개념   pp. 80-81

A   1 dance   2 start   3 enter

B   1 must not   2 will not

C   1 Can you teach me? (O)
     2 May he come in? (O)

D   1 Must, must

혼공연습   pp. 82-83

A   1 must   2 can   3 may   4 must   5 will
     6 may   7 must   8 can

B   1 go   2 visit   3 complete   4 start   5 call
     6 drive   7 finish   8 join

C   1 I will not[won't] call you later.
     2 You cannot[can't] open the door now.
     3 She may not leave early today.
     4 We must not attend the class tomorrow.
     5 She must not know the answer.
     6 We do not[don't] have to clean the room today.

D   1 Can you drive a car?
     2 May she join the meeting tomorrow?
     3 Must he write his report today?
     4 Can we meet them at the café?
     5 Will we finish the assignment soon?
     6 Does she have to go to the doctor tomorrow?

혼공실전 1   pp. 84-87

A   1 prepare   2 call   3 swim   4 leave
     5 finish   6 wear   7 arrive   8 help   9 do
     10 will   11 lead   12 rain   13 clean
     14 meet   15 use   16 complete   17 follow
     18 borrow   19 play   20 attend

B   1 must   2 can   3 may   4 must   5 may
     6 will   7 can   8 must   9 must   10 must
     11 can   12 will

C   1 may not   2 cannot   3 will not
     4 may not   5 will not   6 must not
     7 cannot   8 won't   9 may not   10 will not

D   1 could   2 had to   3 could   4 had to
     5 could   6 had to   7 could   8 had to
     9 could   10 had to

E   1 help, can
     2 May, may
     3 Must, don't have to
     4 go
     5 Will, won't
     6 watch, can't
     7 May, may
     8 Will, will
     9 Can, can

혼공실전 2   pp. 88-91

A   1 can   2 must[should]   3 may[might]
     4 will   5 must   6 may[might]   7 will
     8 must   9 may[might]   10 can
     11 may[can]   12 must[should]

B   1 could   2 had to   3 could   4 had to
     5 had to   6 would   7 could   8 would
     9 had to   10 could   11 would   12 would

C   1 I cannot[can't] finish this task alone.
     2 She may not use my phone.
     3 They must not be poor.
     4 They will not[won't] attend the ceremony
      tomorrow.
     5 We must not[mustn't] waste time on
      unnecessary things.
     6 He could not[couldn't] solve the problem
      yesterday.
     7 She might not come to the party tonight.
     8 You should not[shouldn't] skip your breakfast.

9 I cannot[can't] understand the instructions clearly.

10 You must not[mustn't] forget to lock the door.

11 They will not[won't] agree to our plan.

12 He could not[couldn't] believe the news.

13 She might not see the email.

14 You should not[shouldn't] speak to others that way.

15 He would not[wouldn't] listen to any advice.

D 1 Can you help me?

2 May I leave the class early today?

3 Must we finish all the exercises in the book?

4 Will you attend the workshop tomorrow?

5 Could you explain this concept to me?

6 Did you have to complete the task by yesterday?

7 Do I have to apologize to him for the mistake?

8 Can she play the guitar well?

9 May we use the library after hours?

10 Must he finish the assignment today?

11 Will you open the window for me?

12 Will they visit us this Christmas?

13 Could he solve the problem on his own?

14 Did you have to wake up early yesterday?

15 Would you like some tea?

혼공실전 ㅋ

pp. 92~95

1 ③ 2 ③ 3 ② 4 ⑤ 5 ② 6 ⑤

7 ④ 8 ④ 9 sings → sing 10 ④ 11 ③

12 ① 13 will 14 can 15 may 16 could

17 ⑤ 18 not → do not[don't]

19 had → have 20 does not have to worry

21 May I borrow your book?

22 They must not be strangers. 23 ④

교칙

학생들은 매일 교복을 반드시 착용해야 합니다. 학생들은 수업에 정시에 도착해야 합니다. 학생들은 수업 중에 휴대폰을 사용하면 안 됩니다. 모든 학생들은 숙제를 제시간에 완료해야 합니다. 학생들은 선생님께 언제든 질문할 수 있습니다.

CHAPTER 6
명사와 관사

혼공개념   pp. 98–99

Ⓐ 1 a pencil 2 a dog 3 water

Ⓑ 1 pigs 2 classes 3 mangoes 4 puppies
5 wolves

Ⓒ 1 women 2 children 3 oxen 4 teeth
5 sheep

Ⓓ 1 a 2 an 3 The

혼공연습   pp. 100–101

Ⓐ 1 an apple 2 a car 3 a book 4 joy
5 water 6 New York 7 soap 8 a tree

Ⓑ 1 maps 2 pens 3 boxes 4 flowers
5 desks 6 buses 7 dishes 8 benches
9 churches 10 heroes 11 babies
12 cities 13 countries 14 candies
15 hobbies 16 stories 17 leaves
18 knives 19 lives 20 thieves

Ⓒ 1 feet 2 children 3 men 4 mice
5 geese 6 fish

Ⓓ 1 We need chairs for the event.
2 They watch movies every weekend.
3 My family digs up potatoes.
4 The wind moves branches.
5 She catches dragonflies with her net.
6 I found knives on the floor.

혼공실전 1   pp. 102–105

Ⓐ 1 a cup 2 an umbrella 3 a hat
4 a picture 5 juice 6 a story 7 Honey
8 Milk 9 coffee 10 Suji 11 peace

12 kindness 13 sugar 14 bread
15 trust 16 Ice 17 happiness 18 Seoul
19 an old book 20 sand

Ⓑ 1 Rabbits 2 shoes 3 stars 4 A frog
5 tables 6 flowers 7 rice 8 tires
9 wood 10 flour 11 love 12 presents
13 paper 14 letters 15 gold 16 places
17 air 18 pins 19 Silver 20 honesty

Ⓒ 1 friends 2 classes 3 benches
4 students 5 ladies 6 Foxes 7 copies
8 stories 9 Leaves 10 Typhoons
11 Bananas 12 libraries 13 tomatoes
14 birds 15 armies 16 beaches
17 heroes 18 potatoes 19 pianos
20 photos

Ⓓ 1 clouds 2 jobs 3 geese 4 keys
5 hats 6 race 7 water 8 diaries
9 mice

혼공실전 ㄹ   pp. 106–109

Ⓐ 1 bats 2 planes 3 enemies 4 bones
5 toys 6 brushes 7 fish 8 fireworks
9 women 10 leaves

Ⓑ 1 an 2 a 3 The 4 the 5 The 6 The
7 a 8 The 9 a 10 the 11 The 12 an
13 the 14 a 15 an 16 a 17 an 18 a
19 an 20 an

Ⓒ 1 He collected shells from the beach.
2 She drew fish in her notepad.
3 A chef prepared dishes for his guests.
4 They found footprints in the sand.
5 She caught mice in the attic.
6 She adopted puppies from the shelter.
7 A hunter saw deer in the forest.
8 He bought watches from the market.
9 We saw oxen in the field.
10 A teacher corrected mistakes in the
students' homework.

11 We visited churches built in the 18th century.

12 I could hear echoes in the large cave.

13 A fisherman caught salmon in the river.

14 She found bridges between the two cities.

15 A boy saw witches in his book.

D 1 He used butter to bake the cake.

2 I watched a documentary about Leonardo da Vinci.

3 The soup needs salt.

4 He spilled ink on his notebook.

5 The Colosseum in Rome is an iconic landmark.

6 There wasn't much snow on the road this morning.

7 The Sahara Desert is in North Africa.

8 NASA is planning to send people to Mars.

9 He is full of hope for the future.

10 He has a lot of knowledge about science.

11 Patience is the key to success.

12 She felt deep sadness at that time.

13 Rain can make flowers grow quickly.

14 She wiped the table to remove dust.

15 My sweater is made of soft wool.

혼공실전 ㅋ pp. 110-113

1 ② 2 ② 3 ⑤ 4 ④ 5 a 6 The

7 ② 8 ④ 9 a → an

10 He ordered a loaf of bread.

11 She prepared a bowl of soup 12 ③

13 ⑤ 14 tooth → teeth

15 women → woman

16 I saw a silver ring on the counter.

17 He plays the drum every evening. 18 ①

우리 아빠는 커피 한 잔 마시는 것을 좋아하신다. 그리고 아침에 항상 책을 읽으신다. 가끔은 아침 식사로 달걀을 곁들인 토스트를 드신다. 주말에는 기타를 치며 우리와 함께 노래를 부르신다. 저녁에는 영화를 보거나 책 읽는 것을 좋아하신다.

19 piece → pieces 20 A → The 21 ②

22 ③ 23 ③

옛날 옛적에, 한 농부가 작은 집에 살고 있었다. 어느 날, 그는 나무 아래에서 달걀 하나를 발견했다. 농부는 그 달걀을 집으로 가져가 바구니에 넣었다. 다음 날 아침, 그는 바구니 안에서 황금 달걀을 보았다. 달걀은 아름답게 빛났다. 농부는 그 황금 달걀을 팔아 부자가 되었다.

CHAPTER 7
대명사

혼공개념   pp. 116–117

Ⓐ **1** I   **2** his   **3** me   **4** her

Ⓑ **1** yours   **2** yourself

Ⓒ **1** These are my keys. (○)
  2 It is September 9th. (○)

Ⓓ **1** one   **2** some   **3** any

혼공연습   pp. 118–119

Ⓐ **1** She   **2** his   **3** They   **4** our   **5** me   **6** his
  7 her   **8** us

Ⓑ **1** hers   **2** yours   **3** his   **4** yourself
  5 themselves

Ⓒ **1** These   **2** Those   **3** It   **4** It   **5** It   **6** It

Ⓓ **1** This shirt is small, so I'll buy a bigger one.
  2 The old car was noisy, but this one is quiet.
  3 They have some books for you.
  4 There are some bananas in the basket.
  5 I don't want any dessert after dinner.
  6 Do you have any trouble finding the hotel?

혼공실전 1   pp. 120–123

Ⓐ **1** He   **2** She   **3** They   **4** We   **5** She   **6** I
  7 They   **8** us   **9** her   **10** me   **11** them
  12 him   **13** him   **14** us   **15** her   **16** my
  17 her   **18** his   **19** its   **20** their

Ⓑ **1** mine   **2** yours   **3** his   **4** ours   **5** hers
  6 theirs   **7** hers   **8** ours   **9** theirs   **10** his
  11 myself   **12** himself   **13** himself
  14 herself   **15** ourselves   **16** themselves
  17 himself   **18** herself   **19** himself
  20 myself

Ⓒ **1** This   **2** Those   **3** These   **4** those
  5 this   **6** Those   **7** that   **8** those
  9 These   **10** Those   **11** It   **12** It   **13** It
  14 It   **15** It   **16** It   **17** There   **18** It   **19** It
  20 It

Ⓓ **1** one   **2** any   **3** any, some   **4** some
  5 one   **6** some   **7** any   **8** one   **9** some

혼공실전 2   pp. 124–127

Ⓐ **1** I   **2** She   **3** His   **4** Her   **5** Our   **6** me
  7 them   **8** us   **9** her   **10** him

Ⓑ **1** mine   **2** ours   **3** yours   **4** theirs   **5** hers
  6 his   **7** yourself   **8** herself   **9** ourselves
  10 themselves

Ⓒ **1** I am studying English hard.
  2 He is practicing basketball.
  3 He is waiting for us at the bus stop.
  4 The teacher praised him for his presentation skills.
  5 He left his jacket on the subway.
  6 Thank you for sharing your story with me.
  7 She often visits her grandparents.
  8 The song reminded him of his childhood.
  9 The movie made us laugh so much.
  10 I went to the movies by myself.
  11 He loves ice cream and chocolate.
  12 She asked me several questions.
  13 I think this backpack is his.
  14 You have to solve this problem by yourself.
  15 The gray laptop is hers.

Ⓓ **1** Look at those colorful birds.
  2 That is a very creative idea.
  3 These sunglasses don't match my style.
  4 It takes three hours to get to the hospital.
  5 It will be sunny all weekend.
  6 This muffin is delicious.
  7 I need some water after exercise.
  8 Do you have any questions?
  9 You can take the smaller one.

10 He doesn't have any money in his wallet.

11 It is ten miles from here to the airport.

12 He doesn't have any friends in this town.

13 The teacher gave us some homework.

14 It was foggy this morning.

15 Let's read a fun one.

 혼공실전 3   pp. 128-131

1 ⑤   **2** ④   **3** ①   **4** hers   **5** It   **6** ⑤

7 ①   **8** ③   **9** ⑤   **10** its → their

11 you → yourself   **12** ③

Tom은 그의 엄마를 매우 사랑한다. Tom의 엄마는 매일 그를 돕는다. 그녀는 Tom을 사랑으로 돌본다. Tom은 엄마의 친절에 감사해한다. 그는 엄마에게 감사의 편지를 쓸 것이다.

13 ①   **14** ④   **15** The blue car is not theirs.

16 one   **17** any   **18** some

19 This orange is so fresh and sweet.

20 Those are my favorite songs.   **21** ③

22 (1) His   (2) It   **23** ④

Sam은 내 가장 친한 친구들 중 한 명이다. 어느 날, 그는 나에게 작은 공책을 선물로 주었다. 그는 말했다, "이걸 사용해서 네 생각과 꿈을 써 봐." 나는 매일 밤 자기 전에 그 공책에 글을 쓴다. Sam 덕분에, 이제 나는 내 인생의 이야기를 적을 공간이 생겼다.

CHAPTER 8
의문문

혼공개념   pp. 134-135

A **1** Are   **2** Is   **3** Do   **4** Does   **5** Can

B **1** Who   **2** When

C **1** Where is the bus stop? (O)
  2 How do you bake bread? (O)
  3 Where are your friends? (O)

D **1** Which
  2 isn't, Yes
  3 doesn't, No

혼공연습   pp. 136-137

A **1** Are   **2** Is   **3** Do   **4** Does   **5** Does
  6 Can   **7** Will   **8** Should

B **1** How   **2** Where   **3** When   **4** Who   **5** Why

C **1** Why   **2** Where   **3** What   **4** When
  5 How   **6** Who

D **1** I, am   **2** she, isn't   **3** it, wasn't   **4** I, don't
  5 he, does   **6** they, didn't

 혼공실전 1   pp. 138-141

A **1** Is   **2** Do   **3** Are   **4** Can   **5** Is   **6** Can
  7 Does   **8** Should   **9** Was   **10** Did
  11 Was   **12** Do   **13** Did   **14** Does   **15** Will
  16 Did   **17** Did   **18** Does   **19** Was
  20 Can

B **1** What   **2** Where   **3** Why   **4** When
  5 How   **6** Why   **7** How   **8** What   **9** Who
  10 Why   **11** Who   **12** Who   **13** Why
  14 When   **15** What   **16** What   **17** Where
  18 Where   **19** Why   **20** How

C 1 many 2 long 3 often 4 much 5 long
6 old 7 often 8 far 9 tall 10 many
11 far 12 often 13 far 14 tall
15 often 16 far 17 much 18 long
19 many 20 long

D 1 Which 2 or 3 Which
4 isn't, is
5 is, isn't
6 weren't, were
7 doesn't, doesn't
8 do, do
9 didn't, did

혼공실전 2   pp. 142-145

A 1 Are 2 Is 3 Is 4 Was 5 Can 6 Does
7 Are 8 Do 9 Did 10 Should[Must]

B 1 What 2 Who 3 When 4 Where
5 What 6 How 7 Why 8 Who 9 Where
10 What

C 1 Who is he?
2 What are you doing?
3 Why is she happy?
4 Where is my laptop?
5 Why is the sky blue?
6 How are your parents?
7 What do you want to do?
8 Why does she laugh?
9 Do you know him?
10 How can I help you?
11 Who knows the answer?
12 How old is this tree?
13 When will you graduate?
14 How much water do you drink?
15 How long is the flight?

D 1 don't you, I do, I don't
2 isn't she, she is, she isn't
3 isn't it, it is, it isn't
4 is it, it is, it isn't

5 does it, it does, it doesn't
6 doesn't it, it does, it doesn't
7 didn't he, he did, he didn't
8 did she, she did, she didn't

혼공실전 3   pp. 146-149

1 ① 2 ④ 3 ② 4 ② 5 ⑤ 6 ③
7 When 8 Where 9 How 10 ⑤
11 How 12 ④ 13 and → or
14 How much do you love me?
15 How far is the airport from here? 16 ⑤
17 isn't 18 didn't 19 ④ 20 ① 21 does
22 ② 23 ③

엄마는 항상 나를 사랑하신다. 어느 날, 나는 엄마에게 물었다. "왜 항상 저를 돌봐 주시나요?" 엄마는 미소를 지으며 말하셨다. "너는 내 아이이기 때문이란다." 그리고 나는 물었다. "그럼 엄마는 언제 쉬세요?" 엄마는 웃으면서 말하셨다. "나는 계속해서 쉰단다." 마지막으로, 나는 물었다, "엄마의 모든 사랑은 어디에서 오나요?" 엄마는 내 손을 잡으며 말하셨다. "내 마음에서 온단다." 그녀의 말이 내 하루를 행복하게 만들었다.

혼공
중학 영문법
마스터
Level·1

초판 1쇄 발행   2025년 6월 2일

지은이   허준석
편집   강지희 홍하늘
디자인   박새롬
마케팅   두잉글 사업본부

펴낸곳   혼공북스
출판등록   제2021-000288호
주소   04033 서울특별시 마포구 양화로 113, 4층(서교동, 순흥빌딩)
전자메일   team@hongong.co.kr

혼공북스는 ㈜혼공유니버스의 출판 브랜드입니다.

ISBN   979-11-984935-7-6   13740